<-<-<-<-<-<-<-<-<-<-<-<-<-<-<-<-<-<-<-<-<-<-<-<-<-<-

The Rights of Spring

A MEMOIR OF INNOCENCE ABROAD

David Kennedy

Princeton University Press
Princeton & Oxford

Requests for permission to reproduce material from this work
should be sent to Permissions, Princeton University Press

Published by Princeton University Press, 41 William Street,
Princeton, New Jersey 08540

In the United Kingdom: Princeton University Press, 6 Oxford
Street, Woodstock, Oxfordshire OX20 1TW

LIBRARY OF CONGRESS CATALOGING-IN-PUBLICATION DATA
Kennedy, David, 1954–
   The rights of spring : a memoir of innocence abroad / David
Kennedy.
      p.   cm.
   ISBN 978-0-691-14137-4 (hardcover : alk. paper) —
ISBN 978-0-691-14138-1 (pbk. : alk. paper)   1. Human rights.
2. Human rights advocacy.   3. Human rights advocates.
4. Human rights—Uruguay.   5. Political prisoners—Uruguay.
I. Title.
   K3240.K455 2009
   341.4'8—dc22   2008039006

British Library Cataloging-in-Publication Data is available

This book has been composed in Fournier MT and Din

Printed on acid-free paper. ∞

press.princeton.edu

Printed in the United States of America

10 9 8 7 6 5 4 3 2 1

For Ana, Ramon, Francisco, Victor,

and all those who have allowed

well-intentioned strangers into their

lives, their politics, and their pain.

CONTENTS

AUTHOR'S NOTE   ix

1 Introductions   1

2 Thinking Ahead   10

3 Crossing Over   16

4 Professional Roles   25

5 Direct Examination: Telling Ana's Story   39

6 Cross-Examination: The Doctor's Tale   48

7 The Men of Libertad   58

8 Transition: Preparing to Act   68

9 A Moment of Advocacy   80

10 The Aftermath   85

EPILOGUE   104

AUTHOR'S NOTE

This story begins with a trip I took over spring break many years ago. It was a human rights mission and I was a young law teacher. I have taught and reworked and republished my memories of that adventure several times in the years since. With time, of course, some recollections become sharper, others less so. More striking has been the impact of a changing context for the story. I wrote first when human rights was still largely an enthusiastic, if amateur, affair. The story read and taught quite differently as the human rights movement grew in confidence and institutional power until one could refer easily to the "human rights establishment." Now that the ethical and institutional self-confidence of those years has waned, I have returned to this story to see what might be learned from a look back at those earlier amateur days.

This memoir appeared first, with a lengthy methodological appendix requested by the law review, as "Spring Break," 63 *Texas Law Review*, 1377 (1985). A version was reprinted without the appendix and with a new introduction in *Knowledges: Historical and Critical Studies in Disciplinarity*, edited by Messer-Davidow, Shumway, and Sylvan (University Press of Virginia, 1993) at page 422 and following. A slightly shorter version of the essay appeared as chapter 3 in my *The Dark Sides of Virtue: Reassessing International Humanitarianism* (Princeton University Press, 2004). In publishing it now as a reflection on what has become of the human rights movement, I would like to thank all the readers, students, and colleagues who, over the years, have challenged my story, encouraged me to tell or retell it, and helped me to understand, in quite different ways, what it might mean. I would also like to thank everyone mentioned in the text for sharing the experience, and their own stories, with me. The names of the prisoners have been changed.

The Rights of Spring

1 ✝ INTRODUCTIONS

I met Ana Rivera in the small white clinic at Punta
Rieles prison. The guards stepped outside, I shook
her hand, and Dr. Richard Goldstein, Patrick Bres-
lin, and I became the first outsiders to speak privately
and unconditionally with any of the roughly seven
hundred political prisoners then held in Uruguayan
prisons. We sat down at a small table. Ana was a di-
minutive woman, about twenty-three years old, her
auburn hair pulled awkwardly back in a child's yel-
low plastic barrette. Around each wrist hung a red-
and-white string bracelet. Under her prison overalls,
stenciled boldly with her identification number, she
wore two layers of clothing. Fearing transfer to another prison or judicial proceeding when officials had
come for her some moments before, she had worn
her wardrobe to our brief meeting. Her hands trembled nervously.

Patrick's explanation of our presence was calming. Worn smooth by repetition before numerous officials, his introductory litany of our professions and
affiliations was reassuring, factual, and brisk. I'm a
writer, he's a doctor, and he's a lawyer. We're from
the United States and we represent five scientific
and medical institutions, the New York Academy of

Sciences, the American Public Health Association, the Institute of Medicine of the National Academy of Sciences, the National Academy of Sciences and the American College of Physicians. These became my first one hundred words of Spanish. His next sentence was too long to remember, something like: we have come to Uruguay because these our institutions are concerned about the general health situation among political prisoners in Uruguay and in particular about four medical students arrested almost a year earlier on charges of "subversive association" and a number of other political prisoners reported to be in poor health. Patrick was careful to summarize: "In short, Ana, we have come to speak with you." Dr. Gold-stein will also be happy to discuss any health problems you may have and to examine your body, if you so desire. I think now what I thought as he finished: if only it would last, this moment could be savored, along with so many others just like it from the hey-day of human rights advocacy.

All this happened more than twenty years ago. Uruguay was ruled by military dictatorship. I was a young human rights lawyer, uncertain what to expect. I had visited other prisons, traveled to other continents, but I was very much the amateur, more human rights dilettante than professional, and this was my first time to Uruguay. In those days, the human rights movement itself was a far more ad hoc affair than the complex bureaucracy and professional network it would later become.

Time passed and democracy came to Uruguay. An Uruguayan student told me some years back that one of the prisons we had visited is now a shopping mall. What better testimony to the power of human rights. For a time, the language of human rights was everywhere, while the limits of what it could accomplish and the damage a human rights initiative could sometimes cause were less apparent. American law students yearned to become human rights professionals. Many still do. But in some way the flower has withered; the luster is faded. Though many soldier on, professionals with a cause, the innocence of international human rights has passed. On the one hand, the human rights idea, vocabulary, and movement have become institutionalized, have joined hands with governments, corporations, and all manner of international bureaucracies, foundations, and advocacy groups to legitimate and delegitimate, to spend money, to allocate resources—in short, to exercise power on the global stage. On the other, the heyday of human rights as a common global rhetoric for justice seems to be behind us.

3

It is hard to say why, or how this came about. The two facts seem related—at once more powerful and less innocent, urgent, compelling. Perhaps the movement bit off more than it could chew. There were certainly many disappointments. So many interventions did not work out as we had planned. The vernacular was misused. As an absolute language of righteousness and moral aspiration came to be used strategically, it became less persuasive, easy to interpret as nothing but strategy, cover for political objectives, particular interests clothing themselves in the idiom of the universal. And the politics of the global scene shifted. The Cold War ended and the machinery of human rights focused ever more selectively, in the third world, on Israel, on the axis of evil, and on the remains of the Soviet empire. And then the war on terror intervened, changing the dynamic all over again.

What has become of the first generation of human rights professionals? Some had been liberals of the 1960s, taking their civil liberties commitments onto the global stage. Others, like myself, were children of the seventies for whom Jimmy Carter had made human rights a respectable vernacular for transposing what we remembered of sixties idealism to international affairs in the 1980s. In retrospect, it was an

odd moment. Although the movement traces its ori-
gins and many of its crucial early texts to the end of
World War II, in fact the human rights profession
was launched just as the pendulum swung for a generation toward Thatcher, Reagan, and the politics of
"neoliberalism." Indeed, the rise of human rights
would coincide with that broader enthusiasm for
small states and individual liberties. And as the one
became chastened, so also the other.

As the movement's administrative bureaucracies
grew, many early veterans found themselves sucked
upward from the field to headquarters, to manage-
ment. On a recent visit, I was surprised to find that
Human Rights Watch now takes up several floors in
the Empire State Building, naming and shaming
from a great height. A surprising number of foot
soldiers have left their jobs and written up their stories, stories of early faith confounded, lost amid the
vagaries of politics and context and all the duplici-
ties of good intentions brought to faraway places.
Some, of course, have simply drifted away and find
themselves teaching, lawyering, making policy. Or
working in the many new institutions now at the
forefront of human rights work—trading the revo-
lutionary promise of social justice for the patient in-
crementalism of international tribunals, development

agencies, foundations, or corporate centers for social responsibility.

There is no question that today's professional
humanists, beginners and seasoned veterans alike,
are chastened, pragmatic, and far savvier than we
were then. Painful lessons hard learned have worn
deep grooves and sown nagging doubts about the
dark sides of virtue. There are so many unsavory
things one simply can't do anything about, so many
unsavory things one finds oneself doing in the
human rights business. It all did seem so much sim-
pler then, in Montevideo, in the heyday of human
rights. Democracy was on the rise and we had ring-
side seats. I remember observing a trial in Prague on
a gray and rainy October Tuesday in 1989, in a small
dilapidated courthouse on the outskirts of town,
only to return the following May, flowers in bloom,
for a meeting of Harvard Law School's European
alumni in a newly poshed-up hotel. I asked where
to find the defendant—member of a John Lennon
peace group—whose trial I had sat through, and
was directed to "the Castle." Seems after the Velvet
Revolution he had gone to work in Vaclav Havel's
office, where he was far too busy for an appoint-
ment. Seven or eight of the cut glass goblets I had
bought after the trial to use up the local currency I

had been forced to exchange still survive in my sideboard.

I remember the Uruguay call coming in, just after Christmas—could I head off over spring break? My old friend lowered his voice, a conspiratorial whisper. "This one could be real." Right place, right time, contacts all agreed: we might just make a difference. What did he mean, exactly? We'd get in, see real prisoners, get them out, fly business class? I wasn't exactly sure. But I said OK, sign me up. As I think now about Uruguay and Prague and the many sites where human rights advocates touched down in those years, it is hard not to look back in nostalgia—or with irony. Prisoner of conscience visited, witnessed, perhaps released—this will always be something to celebrate, to relish, to anticipate. But the story of human rights is far sadder, complex, multiple.

Our own story in the Uruguayan prisons that spring is about thinking and doing and struggling, all the while glimpsing so much we did not know, could not see, and do not yet know. Indeed, as Pat stopped talking, things seemed much less clear than they would later appear. Certainly than they appear now, in the way all long-ago events we have not forgotten come to fix themselves in our mind's eye. Indeed, so many years later, I find it hard to reconstruct what

happened with the freshness, the confusion, the uncertainty I experienced. In fact, I find I remember little beyond the stories I have told from time to time
about what happened.

I want to recapture both the confusion of the experience and our efforts to make sense of it, both in Montevideo and later in Boston. At the time, we wanted to
believe. Believe that we were surfing the crest of history, making human rights, enforcing, propagating,
proselytizing, implementing. At the same time, we
wanted to be modest, knowing, savvy—it was all
just a grain of sand, probably dropped in the wrong
ocean.

Once home, what could be told? We had learned.
We had liberated. We had struck a blow. We could
say all that. But we couldn't say we had been turned
on or had gone looking for fun. Even though we had.
Nor did it seem possible to say we had found much in
Montevideo amusing, for who could know whether
we were laughing in irony or mocking the suffering
of the innocent? The first years after we came back
were serious years for legal scholarship and professional debate. Identity politics, political correctness,
a liberal academy on the defensive, tearing itself
apart. There was much about a trip like ours that
could not be said, or heard. In the first months after

I returned, the *Harvard Law Review* accepted a version of this story, but as the editing went on, they got
cold feet. It wouldn't look right, for them, for me.
There was something unseemly about uncertainty in
the face of suffering. To write about moral ambiguity risked sacrilege.

Today, the audience can hear different things—
demands different things. We expect accounts of
well-meaning ventures to be ironic, ambivalent, and
self-questioning. Twenty years later, it is terribly
hard not to say we saw it all then, the chaos, the complexity, the dark sides. But this is also not true. We
were serious and lacked the distance to understand
how an entire generation could have been blown so
far off course in our simple quest for justice and a
more humane world. Where we felt ambivalence and
confusion, we could report the feelings and our first
efforts to make sense of them. For all the movement
has matured in the years since the three of us went to
Montevideo, I do not think we have yet pounded this
common ambivalence and confusion, excitement,
boredom, and occasional vague nausea into common
sense. There remains much we might learn from the
impressions of an amateur, before the spectacular rise
and subsequent decline of the international human
rights movement.

In the event, as we got going, Ana trembled less, and the three of us shifted in our chairs, relaxing. Still, it was terribly hard to see where things were headed, or to figure out exactly what we should do next. To move forward we needed to push our time into meaning, transforming ourselves and Ana into characters and our encounter into a story. As we interviewed Ana and other prisoners, and returned to our hotel to plot our next moves, we wove these moments into narratives about our institutions, our professions, the changing Uruguayan political scene, our mission, and ourselves. Having transformed the experience into narrative just to orient ourselves as we continued, we had little to rely on afterward to understand just what had, in fact, happened. We re-told the stories. And we unraveled them. But either way, the experience seemed to melt away. Just what had happened, who were we, and what had we done?

2 ⚡ THINKING AHEAD

Six days before meeting with Ana, I had left Boston amid the half-joking admonitions of friends to stay out of trouble. As we drove through the Callaghan

Tunnel to Logan Airport, our mood was jocular. Uruguay seemed far away: dangerous, exotic, exciting. So long as we kept it distant, Uruguay seemed able to bear the burden of our excitement. As spring vacation approached, I had felt drawn by anything elsewhere, by the prospect of new people and different problems, by the possibility that in Uruguay I would feel more like an international lawyer than I did grading midterm papers on the living room floor. I might be granted a different kind of respect from what I was accorded in my habitual workplace environment. Although I would be gone only two weeks, I knew time would move differently, more intensely, more quickly, and, lost in new details, I would sharply break the semester's continuity. With luck, I might even return tanned. Uruguay occupied a difficult position; it would need to remain foreign to excite me and to sustain my identity as an American and a human rights lawyer, and yet disclose to me its secrets, satisfy the attraction that brought me there.

Waiting at Logan for my flight to be called, I described my plans to friends who would remain behind. Despite the rush of adrenaline these fantasies produced, I felt a nagging doubt. The more remote I imagined Uruguay to be, the more I doubted whether

11

I had anything to offer it. A doubt surfacing first as a political question of standing. What "right" did I have to do this to "them?" So long as I pictured Uruguay and myself as different enough to sustain my excitement, I worried about becoming an agent of "cultural imperialism." Yet if I were not so different, I would never have been invited. If I could believe that I had a right to go, or even a duty, constructing a formula from which I could derive some limit and basis for my interference as well as some expectation about my effectiveness, my doubts would fade. I could at once respect and contain our mutual difference in a familiar framework of rights and duties.

The complement of this noble doubt, of course, was fear. I worried that I would find Uruguay disorienting, unsettlingly different, outside both my competence and my legitimate involvement. But more than that, such worries—about standing, entitlement, credentials—are also evidence of unease about precisely the experience of free responsible decision, the exercise of political judgment, the wielding of power, the allocation of stakes. Intervention in the world is scary. It would be so much easier if it were not I who acted, but my institutions. If it were not my decision to intermeddle, but my right, my duty, my job.

Sitting aboard our Varig flight, Richard and I care-
fully memorized and shredded background documents detailing the Uruguayan human rights scene
from various legal and political perspectives. We
hoped that the information from these documents
would arm us in Montevideo, keep us from being
duped, and empower us to confront, interrogate, and
understand. But we did not want to take them with
us. Who knew what might jeopardize our intention
to float through the official scene buoyed by our reasonable demeanors and institutional affiliations? The
documents might disarm us, marking us as foreign,
dangerous interlopers just as we sought to assimilate.
By destroying the documents while preserving their
power for us, we reassured ourselves that we could
remain sufficiently innocuous to establish common
ground with Uruguayan officials without sacrificing
our ability to oppose their regime. Finding a way to
seem unthreatening yet potent adversaries would be
a recurring problem.

Talking with students about this scene in the
years since, I have watched the rise and fall of worry
about cultural interlopery. For a time, self-confident
agents of universal norms seemed untroubled by
doubt; it was hard for them to understand my worry.
In other years the entire group would be gripped by

the willies to the point of paralysis. For economic development, everything; for cultural change or political engagement, nothing. Let us listen to them, to
their priorities: we come and go only to serve. Let us
grant, and honor, their sovereignty. And then this
deference would come in turn to seem meek, contra-
dictory, pathetic. As a group, my students would be
drawn to procedural fixes—perhaps we should en-
sure that they are well represented, fight for their
participation. But then somehow no procedure seems
up to it, no representative persuasive. They are represented and things aren't getting any better. Perhaps
it is we who must represent the unrepresented; suddenly the class revives with bravura. The odd thing
is how these sentiments ebb and flow like fashion, the
mark less of an attitude toward the other than of a
common professional, generational sensibility. Talking about the scene, members of the group encourage
one another, draw back together, console, reassure
that we know, that we must, and then as quickly that
we know not, dare not.

Participating in these discussions, I've become
ever more convinced that we must learn to embody
the will to power, confess our politics to ourselves.
If you don't want to rule the world, I tell students,
why are you taking this course? After all, politics

denied is never no politics at all. Saying this chal-
lenges, confronts, can often recruit. For all we think
about human rights work as naming, shaming, and
confronting faraway bad guys, my own most difficult—and, I hope, productive—confrontations in
the world of human rights have come back at home.
In Montevideo, the confrontations were of a very
different sort, and, more often than not, just what we
didn't need. With one another, or with those we
would meet.

By our fourth day on the ground, as we approached
Punta Rieles, Richard, Pat, and I thought we knew
each other pretty well. Although we had much still
to learn about Uruguay, the three of us seemed to
have become a close team. In three days of intense
negotiations, we had developed a comfortable division of labor. The writer introduced us, translating,
explaining, clarifying. The doctor spoke for our institutions, enunciating our compassionate concerns,
setting forth our objectives. I tried to make sure
that the agenda for each meeting was completed and
our demands were clearly presented. Yet the more
smoothly we worked together, the more comically
reductionist it sounded to hear Patrick described as a
"writer from Washington," or Richard as the "doctor from New York."

3 ⅋ CROSSING OVER

Puenta Rieles prison stood on a slight rise at the end of a long driveway, somewhat off a main highway out of Montevideo behind a poor settlement. As it became visible at a distance behind a low fence, it resembled a small redbrick sanatorium near my hometown in southern Michigan where my high school church group had played bingo with the patients. We passed smoothly through the checkpoints despite our early arrival. Guards examined our documents, more formally and seriously than thoroughly. Someone looked in the trunk. Gates opened, and we drove up a freshly raked white gravel drive toward the main entrance. Off to the left stood a small barracks with eighteen or twenty off-duty soldiers gawking at us from its front steps. Two junior officers walked smartly to the gate to meet our car.

For me, we seemed to have reached the final boundary separating our mission from its object. Our passage into Uruguay had taken us across a series of borders. Each ritual of entry, through a customs portal at the Montevideo airport or into the office of a government official, had both strengthened our sense of solidarity and reassured us that we were making contact with Uruguay. Each time we were confronted

with a man who emerged from the background of
Uruguayan life, cast suddenly in the role of gate-
keeper. Often as we crossed such a boundary we found
common ground, momentarily suspending our identities. Sometimes we argued, pleaded, or tricked our
interlocutor into letting us pass. Usually we simply
presented documents. When we presented and imagined ourselves as our passport identities, as generic
professional and procedural conformists, we nor-
mally felt no particular relationship to the men who
emerged to usher us in. Nor, it seemed, did our identities shift as we passed from one side to the other.

This time, however, as we stepped from the car in
front of the prison gates, the boundary crossing
seemed threatening and confusing. To our bemuse-
ment, the government had provided us with a blond,
miniskirted guide in addition to a blue Peugeot and a
driver. As she emerged from the car to curious stares
from the barracks crowd, I realized that she was the
only woman in sight. Surrounded by men with ma-
chine guns, the women's prison secreted its female
charges from view. Standing in the sun watching our
guide step gracefully from the Peugeot, I feared that
my desire to see the women prisoners, to cross the
boundary guarded by these men, shared something
with their prurient fascination for our guide.

Was it wrong to think that? I didn't think so then. In the intensity of identity politics, the flash of feminist anger that shot through the campuses in the following years, I was told I should not have thought it. What, moreover, about my interest in the guards, the "homosocial" in boundary crossing, as we would come to call it? As the emotional intensity of these reactions has waned, it has become easier to understand how boundaries and identities are made, and assaulted, and reconfigured in moments like this. Stepping up to the prison, I was thinking about women and men, the contrast somehow bringing to consciousness the liminal moment of crossing over, when the mundane fact of made boundaries becomes momentarily visible. In prejudice and expectation, ritual and desire.

Pat and I shed our professional accoutrements. Legal documents, cameras, notepads. Richard tucked his medical bag beneath the car seat, turning back to slip a stethoscope into his pocket. I wanted to be inconspicuous and open to whatever might confront us on the other side, and Richard wanted to prepare.

Both young officers greeted us warmly. The leaner, who was clearly in charge, ushered us past a statue of Artigas, ubiquitous sign of Uruguayan nationalism, and into the warden's office where we received smiles, handshakes, and coffee. Smartly pressed but curious soldiers milled outside the door. We sat down for an exchange of formalities. Rituals of boundaries and bonding.

As I fingered the tassels of the leopard-skin antimacassar I found draped across the black leather arm of my chair, topped with a copper ashtray, Pat identified us: names, professions, institutional affiliations. The warden seemed unsure how to treat his first international delegation. He was visibly proud of his office, its order, his officers' demeanor. Pat described our object: we want to confirm the health of one medical student "in whose case our sponsors are interested," and of five other prisoners "reported to be in ill health." Does the warden believe that this is really our object? Is it slightly plausible—to him, to us—that five American institutions would "become interested" in particular prisoners? Although I realize that defining interests this way might free us from anything but professional detachment, I wonder whether Pat has put the assertion too matter-of-factly. Perhaps he should tell a story about how institutions like ours get interested in cases like this and send delegations such as this to prisons like his. The proceduralist in me wants a better articulation of our standing. My mind wanders—why did they send us here? Who are *they* anyway—I had not met our New York clients.

I notice the younger officer nodding seriously, as if he were checking the text of Pat's speech against his delivery. I am relieved. Maybe we all share a comfortable distance from Pat's remarks, and the officer understands that this is merely our handle. Perhaps he talks about his prison's having "taken an interest" in this or that when he is downtown. Maybe these "interests" are what we and they care about.

In any case, everyone is determined to play this script to the hilt. We explain that our concern is scientific and our motivation humane. We are interested in public health, not public policy. (I wonder as I make this bald assertion what it could mean in such circumstances to say that public health and public policy are distinct. On the other hand, if our institutions did not think we could keep them separate, would they have sent us on this mission?) Richard agrees with the warden that we will see the medical student for a substantial period of time, the other prisoners only long enough to ascertain their health. The duration of our contact with each prisoner will be determined by the theory we have used to justify interest in her case and access to her presence. But does a physical exam really take less time than a symbolic interrogation?

Although it might scare the warden off were we to do otherwise, I wonder whether we are right to deny interest in other prisoners, treating our Washington-based list of the sick as definitive. Perhaps we could ask for more: more prisoners, more access, more time. But it appears that the hollower the story of our institutional motivation sounds, the easier it is to get the warden's cooperation and the smoother our relations seem. His superiors have authorized him to grant these specific requests, and he is relieved when we press on him no other demands.

As the warden takes over the conversational initiative, he builds upon the common ground that Pat has established. He describes the prison clearly and proudly. He appears to assume that everyone appreciates a well-run detention facility. I nod sincerely. I picture him, reduced to a stereotype, expounding this story to his wife over dinner. Perhaps he is standing by a piano. I flash on a movie, about Germans, about Auschwitz. I begin to wonder about that flash, as metaphor, as wish, while he explains that we must understand that these are violent prisoners, threatening the Uruguayan community.

I hope he knows that our conversation is ceremonial and that my acquiescence signals only my foreknowledge of the text he is reciting. As he continues,

I begin to fear that we may betray the prisoners before we see them by associating ourselves too completely with his authority. But surely they will understand that I recognize that he must say this, accept that he wants to say it, that he believes it, and that our silence is in their interest. This is just trickery, just a ceremony, men's talk. Perhaps I think, "When it's over, ladies, I will be true to you." The warden continues. Because they are violent, these individuals have been segregated in this more secure facility. He neatly reverses the violence, projecting it into the prisoners. I notice the nineteenth-century military portraits behind the warden's desk, signs of institutional continuity in this comfortable office. One of the portraits resembles the gaunter of the two junior officers. Young, soft—there is indeed no violence here. These men are managers.

I begin to suspect that the warden must be convinced, not that we buy his arguments, but that we will respect his assertions, taking them without challenge. This is his office, and his characterization of the situation will stand. We are just passing through; our offices are far away. My nodding becomes vigorous, even understanding. Perhaps our institutions understand their institutions. Perhaps nodding is my standing. As I nod on, Richard sits forward and begins to

interrupt the warden's lecture. The initiative passes
to us.

My instinct now is to spar with the warden. As-
suming a demeanor of factual curiosity, I ask how
violent prisoners are selected for segregation here:
on the basis of their crime, their particular acts,
some other factor? The warden explains, as we already knew from our shredded documents, that only
those accused of crimes against the state are here,
even if they have not been convicted or are accused
merely of association or spoken criticism. We let the
contradiction pass. Why are we speaking with him
anyway—what is this conversation? The warden re-
claims the initiative, playing on our insecurity about
interfering in Uruguayan affairs. We rest obsequious
while he explains that in the Uruguayan context, political criminals are the dangerous social threats. He
recommends two books on national security and the
role of the Uruguayan military in case we have any
questions.

Twenty years on, I wonder what became of our
warden. Did some transitional justice procedure re-
educate him to our universal perspective, offer him
some peace? Was he made to suffer, that he might be
released from suffering? This man, this manager:
perhaps he was hoisted up, hair shorn, before his

enemies. Did they go too far? Or perhaps he moved to the suburbs, sold furniture, raised his family, retired, died. Did he remain, in all the years that have passed, the same self, any more than I? If he was brought to account, by his son, his neighbors, by Ana and her parents, her boyfriend, something in me wishes him well. Whether he offered apologies, felt regret, or stuck with timid self-justification, rigidity, and professionalism, it all now seems to slip through my fingers, so paltry as an accounting of responsibility, the product of a later story, a later audience. Responsibility was for then. As for the strange way all of us are separate, if he can live with it, I can too. I hope, given the chance, I would choose not to take responsibility for desiring his confession, his punishment, his enlightenment.

I hope Ana has found peace, love, power. Though I must say, she seemed remarkably at peace when we met, in love, her life transformed by her exercise of power. I would not want to freeze her in a story of suffering that could be unlocked only by some confession from the man who was once her warden. Doing so would make her live her time in prison forever, would render our warden a strange frog-prince, alone able to grant her closure and set her free. I have changed her name, and those of all the

24

prisoners. I hope they will simply have floated free. As for the warden, in the end I should probably leave it here: he was nice to us that day, though I noted no conspiratorial wink of solidarity.

In his office, the conversation turned. We have heard, I tell him, that the prison routine at Punta Rieles and Libertad is intended to break down the prisoner's personality structures. I expect he will rebut by protesting that the routine is necessitated by bureaucratic considerations, a protest that would allow him to feel justified while underscoring the banality of the prisoner's suffering, permitting us each to feel satisfied by the exchange. To give him this chance, I ask about running a high-security prison— how does he determine the measures necessary to deal with such criminals? Without hesitation he breaks the cultural barriers between us with a broad smile, acknowledging with pride that he learned what he knows from the American military who trained him.

4 ⵟ PROFESSIONAL ROLES

In a way, edging toward Punta Rieles, we were just actors playing parts in a tale made familiar by hundreds of childhood fantasies. We were grounded in fealty to our sponsoring institutions and bound by the oaths of our professional service. We hoped that, like knights abroad, we would band together warmly in foreign territory, our friendships tested and forged. But, in another way, we were more than just actors in a familiar cultural drama. Whether in remaking our institutional sponsorship, redefining our professional roles, or developing our team spirit, we were also narrators and directors, creating our roles and casting others as we wished in a production staged against the backdrop of Ana's imprisonment.

There are few human rights activists without sponsors. Activism is, in this sense, a representational activity. More often today the sponsor is a professional, institutional entity, established precisely to send human rights professionals off into the world, to gather testimony, to name and shame. At the time, many professional institutions of other types were toying with taking a stand, becoming involved. Unsurprisingly, not every potential institutional patron is anxious to send would-be activists charging into battle. Both the institutionalization of sponsorship and the old scramble for the credentials of patronage mean that action, even when guided by the activist's intuition or inspired by his faith, refers back to the institution's motive and forward to its goal. In this sense, the activist merely implements. At the beginning, it was often quite ad hoc, teams assembled for this or that. Today it has become a profession. What we had to do to one another, to ourselves, to become a team, is now done by institutions, law faculties, internships, placement offices.

Transforming Pat, Richard, and me from Writer in Washington, Doctor in New York, and Lawyer in Boston to writer-doctor-lawyer in Montevideo required imagination on the part of our sponsoring institutions, which initially regarded sending missions to Montevideo as somewhat outside their normal portfolio. Their long-standing concern for the plight of foreign colleagues needed to be translated into an "interest" in four specific Uruguayan medical students and a willingness to send three activists out on their trail. In those days, scientific institutions often resisted engaging in human rights work because they feared it would diminish their scientific neutrality— ironically the very neutrality that might enable and legitimize their human rights work. It was not yet clear that human rights was ideologically safe, spoken in the name of a universal quite widely acceptable to their peers, as professionally sound as their scientific research.

Professional associations often resisted this work
because they feared they would have little to offer. It
seems counterintuitive, if not a little perverse, to
think of political surveillance and imprisonment as
threats to the confidentiality of the doctor-patient relationship, of systematic torture as a deterioration in
the public health system. Moreover, scientists, like
other professionals whose routine work seems far
from politics and deep in expertise, often fear that
they will appear naive or out of place in the hurly-
burly of human rights work. I have often heard some
of the best-educated young people in the world
demur when asked how the world might be made
more just—we really don't know enough; we're not
qualified, not ready for rulership.

Overcoming these doubts is not simply the tri-
umph of action over the passive habits of professional
fuddy-duddies, however attractive that image might
be. Among our sponsors, these doubts were over-
come primarily through reliance on well-worn norms
of professional responsibility to limit and channel
what could be done, against the background of a ris-
ing confidence in the universality of human rights
ideology. Precisely, in other words, by claiming that
torture *was*, has always been and must always be,
a matter of public health. And, of course, it is no

28

different to claim that inflicting this or that pain *is* "torture," when your institutional mandate marks torture as your concern. Pat, Richard, and I moved to action in different ways, by learning to think of ourselves as professionals, as writer/doctor/lawyer, and to imagine how such a professional might make Ana and her compatriots suitable objects for our moral outrage.

As a young academic without tenure, I worried about becoming involved. Would it seem too political? As a professional experience, would it seem too remote? When I got back, I shared my experience with a senior colleague who specialized in questions of professional responsibility, client confidentiality, obligations to the court, thinking something of what we had done might resonate. But it was all too far away—it was hard to think how a Code of Professional Responsibility crafted with great care for lawyering at home could guide thinking about a prison, still less a torture chamber, so far south of the equator.

But Harvard Law School, where I worked, had also been moving toward a public commitment to "international human rights" and the establishment of a "program." There was some tension about it—should it focus on research, or also entertain the

possibility of advocacy? If advocacy, how would the
Harvard name, logo, be deployed? In those days, the
faculty shared the sense that any institutional participation in advocacy could threaten the faculty's academic freedom. The micro-politics of first movers
and holdouts and of the rather sudden shift to con-
sensus that human rights advocacy was the ultimate
expression and defense of academic freedom rather
than a threat to it would be another story. Whatever
the process, over time, foreign advocacy, human
rights advocacy, came to seem a neutral enough defense of the "rule of law" to make institutional support possible, until students were rushing off in every
direction with each vacation. This was not a choos-
ing up of sides—indeed, as the years went by, we
tended to use the rubric of "human rights" to refer to
everything from foreign investment to cultural revolution. Nevertheless, international human rights
work promised safely distanced contact with the cer-
tifiably barbaric, while seeming the natural extension
of an institutional commitment to civil rights, professional responsibility, and the rule of law.

Taken together, these images rendered institutional
support for human rights activism possible. They
also gave that activism a certain structure. The activists were to be dispatched as professional, individual

advocates deployed upon a foreign context in service of something quite general: "international human rights." In Uruguay we were looking for two kinds of people, clients and abusers. It is not simply that we figured Uruguay as both familiar and barbaric, but that we sought in Uruguay a terrain on which we could identity and link the two through our professional language and role. In one sense, after all, doing so made Uruguay a quite familiar place. When we script the barbarian as a "rights abuser" and the victim as our "client," we do render the strange familiar. Moreover, we now have a role in Uruguay: to "represent" the client against the abuser. In this fantasy, there is a missing third—the judge, before whom we denounce, who will enforce the norms we articulate, punish the violations we prove or bring to light.

This missing third, the eye and sword of judgment, kept unsettling us. It often arose as a worry about our effectiveness—in a way, the flip side of worry about standing. After we had found the facts, would our institutions return like avenging angels? Would the "international community"? Was history on our side? What had our warden to fear? Or might we perhaps rely on the better conscience of our interlocutors, treat them at once as criminal, judge, and jury? In the years since, the urgency of these questions has led human rights practitioners to construct an entire Potemkin village of international courts and tribunals, stage props to instill the fear of retribution when activists speak in the name of norms. In Uruguay, our double struggle for a plausible mandate and an effective promise that our mission would one day find its completion channeled our concerns about violence into a vernacular we could pin to our sponsors—public health and law. This transformed our interest in Uruguayan politics into a physical examination of Ana's body, our outrage into a dispassionate recounting of rights violated, remedies not provided.

An activist's mission is shaped by the oaths of his professional service as much as by his institutional origin. There seem to be few human rights activists who do not enter the field as something: as Christian witness, concerned citizen, public health worker, lawyer. To feel at home in human rights work and to become successful in the field often require only that an activist become better at playing such a role. As a result, action occurs through the prism of these identities. It is, after all, the "activist" who acts.

In the warden's office, our roles seemed like stepping-stones across the cultural divide, simplifying our relations, rendering them possible, closing out the distracting issues raised by unstructured thinking about our situation. We could communicate as Doctor to Lawyer through Writer-Translator to Warden. But our roles produced new walls between us as well as intimacies and complicities. Often I feared that our roles would trap us in wooden sterility or render us complicit in our prisoners' dilemma, even as I counted on them to facilitate direct human contact.

It is not so easy to cast aside a professional identity. No more for us than for those we met. An edifice of roles is not simply a prison for our imagination, nor ought we simply to romanticize confronting one another more directly. At Punta Rieles, I tried to picture the warden dining at home, hoping to give voice to the desk plaque that announced his name: Kleber Papillon. David and Kleber relaxing around that piano. Sherry. Wives lounging on couches. Servants spreading dinner. My effort at empathy had placed us in a television miniseries aired the previous fall, precisely because I, the foreign lawyer, would never find him revealed, no longer the warden. The best I could do was to write a soap-opera husband into the script in his place. No matter how many Klebers I imagined, I was simply imagining a difference from "warden," perhaps a private man, a husband, off duty.

As warden, Papillon had to defend his prison while also letting us in, an admission that belied his defense. Richard had to cast his concerns in the language of medical ethics, for his role was that of doctor, an identity his presence in this remote political prison belied. But these scripts were much more open than these structural tensions suggest. To me, Papillion's name and title were more repositories than identities. When I spoke to "Kleber Papillon," I placed his violence elsewhere, in his profession, his institution, his service. On the other hand, when we connected as professionals sipping coffee, I placed the violence in Papillon or his men, in the rough edges of his silken intention to help us. Working with this ambiguity— now Papillon, now the warden—I avoided both blaming the prisoners for the violence against them and openly rebuking Warden Papillon's account of their suffering. One might analyze our coffee klatch flirtation as complicity or shrewdness, measure it against the greater complicity of accord or the greater opposition of rebuking him directly, but the play was simply more ambiguous, more tenuous, more shifting than such accounts suggest.

Meanwhile, if relations with the warden seemed wooden, getting to know one another as a team seemed unambiguously human. Indeed, it was by contrast to our own solidarity that relations with the Uruguayans seemed satisfactorily distanced and professional. Yet banding together on foreign soil, like relating to our Uruguayan counterparts, was itself a more ambiguous affair than it seemed. We became friends, but that friendship also developed out of a fluid role-play.

Our delegation had been constructed around our diverse professions, and indeed we fell easily into a stereotypical division of labor. I, the lawyer, became responsible for aggressive formality; Richard, the doctor, for compassionate bedside manners. Patrick, the writer-translator, mediated, interpreted, and explained. After a while we joked about the writer who refused to travel without his doctor and lawyer. This joke, by reducing our roles to tools that might be taken up and discarded as we thought fit, helped release the discomfort we felt about behaving in such stereotypical professional ways. Although we were glad for the release, that did not mean we transcended our roles completely. Nor did we want to. And neither, as it turned out, did the simple opposition between roles and selves capture the complexity of our relationships. We came to know one another by playing with our sense of one another as Patrick-Richard-David and as writer-doctor-lawyer.

In this play, we posited one another as roles and as differences from roles. I came to know Richard as "Richard" by contrast to "the Doctor," yet the characteristics associated with each seemed fluid. Sometimes Richard seemed more firm than my image of the compassionate doctor, and I knew him by contrast to his role. Sometimes, when he seemed too nice, I knew him as a doctor, whose compassion was required for the triad doctor-lawyer-writer. But my image of doctors was fluid—they seemed both compassionate healers and dispassionate scientists. Which was Richard? Whichever he was, both were projections of my own interpretive imagery. And I am sure he came to know me by interpreting my behavior both within and against his notions about lawyers. Repeated in all the permutations three people and three roles can generate, these experiences were what "becoming friends" meant.

As we related both to one another and to the warden, we shifted among roles—now I was the lawyer, now David; now he was the warden, now Papillon. Throughout, we deferred the moment at which we would settle our identities. Indeed, our ability to relate both to one another and to the warden depended upon our ability to defer the moment at which we would choose to be just the doctor, the lawyer, or the writer, or to treat our opposite number as simply a warden.

Usually, telling stories about our activities is supposed to settle issues left open in the experience. In analyzing my time with the warden, however, I seem able to decide whether he was a dutiful warden or a nice guy only by treating some detail of our interaction as dispositive: he offered us coffee; he grimaced menacingly. In this way activism avoids ambiguity by reference to an analysis that treats the ambiguity as having already been resolved in action. Yet just as the patterns we embroider onto our relations are undone when the ambiguity of the experience is recaptured, so the ambiguity of our analyses is belied by the felt authenticity of our experiences.

Oddly, this work—weaving meaning into our lives only to rip out the cloth—is forgotten, and the story seems simply to unfold, to progress. Propelled by our practice and reimagined by our analysis, time seems to move forward independent of our activities. Moreover, as we forget the ambiguity of our play, the results of our activities come to seem real. Papillon was and had always been a warden when our team arrived. What began as a play that we made came to seem like life itself. As a result, while playing with one another's identities, we came to feel that we were manipulating real boundaries and transcending real differences that preexisted our work.

For all its ambiguity, as both lived and told, our story seemed to have direction and meaning. In one sense, the origin lay with our sponsors, the direction provided by fantasies of our own effectiveness, the return of order, the end of history. In another, more palpable sense, however, direction and meaning were both provided by Ana. The promise of access to Ana gave significance to our work, and the prospect of meeting Ana shaped our relations with each other and with the Uruguayan officials. Meeting her was our goal; to have met her would be the warden's repudiation, the violence done to her body the Archimedean point around which our entire play turned. When we found ourselves connecting with Papillon emotionally, rather than just professionally, it was fealty to Ana that made us reconstitute him as warden, reassert our difference. When we differentiated ourselves from the warden, it was a sense of our shared difference from Ana that rejoined our team to Papillon. Ana shaped our relations, ordered our experience, gave our mission significance and meaning. And now we had met.

5 ⚸ DIRECT EXAMINATION: TELLING ANA'S STORY

After our introduction, Ana asked Pat what we wanted to know. A moment of fumbling silence. Pat, Richard, and I had planned our interrogation. We had known that time would be short and conditions uncertain. We had worried that the prisoners might have been too well briefed or might be too frightened to speak freely. We had thought that we would need to "establish trust" and move quickly to get what we needed. Richard was a doctor: he needed some health history and we needed to leave time for a brief physical exam. I was a lawyer: I needed details of the arrest, incarceration, and defense. Our interrogation would have to pass through Pat's simultaneous translation. We acknowledged, of course, that the client-patient-prisoner should be able to tell his-her-its own story. That was sometimes necessary, we knowingly reassured one another, before one could get a direct response to questions, and it might uncover something we would not have thought to ask. Thinking like a lawyer, however, I realized that open-ended questioning, like other luxuries of a relaxed interrogation, would have to give way to direct questioning under such difficult conditions as these.

Despite this fairly clear sense of the professionally necessary, doubt seeped into my demeanor as we began. Perhaps because I was uncertain about our standing—we were, after all, only self-styled doctor and lawyer for these people—I wondered whether a more relaxed conversation might not be better. Hadn't we just interrogated the warden? Should we use the same skills on Ana? At the same time, I worried that just this ambivalence might combine with difficult interviewing conditions to sabotage our ability to obtain the information that later would turn out to be important.

Richard told Ana we had about an hour together and asked her to begin by telling us about her arrest and the subsequent events that led to her arrival at Punta Rieles. Good approach, I thought; chronological. With so little time, her story has to make sense. If it rambles, she might not cohere. Ana, calming now, seems to know exactly how to proceed. As she picks up Richard's invitation, she seems to me to have prepared several stock cassettes for such an interview, dry factual renditions of her arrest, treatment, prison life, student politics, and Uruguayan militarism. My fears about reticent or inarticulate prisoners, which Ana's trembling hands had rekindled, now fade. I stop staring and listen.

She had been arrested on June 13, 1983, while walking on the street alone near her boyfriend's flat. I start taking notes. Officers put her in a car and took her to the police station at about 4:00 p.m. She relates some details about her boyfriend. He, too, is a medical student. They met ... I steer her back: what did they tell her when they put her in the car? Did they take any documents or possessions? She responds nicely—nothing, no, but they ransacked her boyfriend's flat, picking up some literature from the medical school student council. What happened at the police station? I inject the questions softly through Pat, recording her responses seriously. Smooth so far. Her boyfriend is now in prison at Libertad. I realize that we will be seeing him later in the day. I begin to think of Ana as a student activist; her calm willingness to speak seems to reflect a self-assured politicization. She says that she never advocated violence and renounces it, contrary to charges made at the police station. As her demeanor reassures, my mind wanders from her words. Although I suppose I called forth this stereotype, it begins to bore me. I think about her boyfriend, wonder how they got together, whether they discussed the possibility of imprisonment, separation. But I ask about the police station again: who said what when?

Richard, less bored than impatient, interrupts—
perhaps we should just let her narrate. I stop but feel
a bit uneasy about abandoning my campaign for the
legally relevant facts. Our need for this specific information stemmed more from our desire to be their
doctor and lawyer than from something intrinsic to
our representation. Perhaps our institutional sponsors needed to have certain information to remain
interested in the cases, in the mission, to feel successful. Perhaps they even had a right to certain information, having sent us so far. Luckily, my insecurity
gives way to resignation. Maybe it's hopeless to try
to get all the information we want. I'm not really
their lawyer, after all. Her own story, I imagine, will
at least be more interesting.

Ana skips ahead to her first days of incommuni-
cado incarceration. The chronology is broken, although her story remains familiar from background
reports. But suddenly there is no cassette. She reports
being blindfolded, doused in cold water, forced to
stand in unheated and drafty surroundings, arms and
legs outstretched. An electric prod is applied to her
fingers, toes, eyes, nose, mouth, and genitals. She is
tied to a metal bed frame; electrodes are fastened
to her face, genitals, and extremities. Someone cranks
a hand-operated generator. She can hear it. The

cranking stops and resumes. Her hands, wrapped in cloth, are tied behind her back. She is hoisted by her wrists and suspended. As she hangs, they strike and prod her. She wakes up on the ground near a stair. Still blindfolded, she hears a medic cautioning the torturer about head injury. The hanging, the electricity, the torture are repeated.

On June 28 the torture ends and she appears before a judge, charged with membership in the Communist Party. She has signed a confession and a statement that she has been well treated. The police return her to the police station and allow her to contact her family for the first time. On August 4 she is brought to Punta Rieles where she remains awaiting trial.

We have spent forty-five minutes together and still have not discussed the prison, her health, or her defense. But somehow in the last few minutes I have lost interest in the case; I find her personal story too intimate and shocking to relate to. Ana stops talking and Pat looks to me for more questions. I am fascinated by the strings around her wrists, stare at them, want to admire them, inquire about their origin.

Richard asks about her health. They discuss several medical complaints. Ana describes the prison regimen. Her tone is flat, matter-of-fact. My mind holds and cannot release the image of electrodes on her wrists; tries to, but cannot, visualize a hundred volts surging on her lips as she speaks. As Richard begins a physical exam, I leave the room. I have become the lawyer again. The doctor will view the body. Outside, in the hallway, the young officer who had accompanied us to the examining room stands chatting with a group of female infirmary personnel. His uniform is smart beside their sacklike smocks. I straighten my tie. The autumn sun lights the group through the bars of an open window. The officer flirts with a nurse. She touches his cheek. They laugh.

We spoke with five other women that morning, all of whom had been at Punta Rieles longer than Ana and had been reported to have had health problems. All reported torture. The wrists of one young woman showed the scars of a recent suicide attempt. Another, whom I had taken for sixty as she described her fourteen years in prison, her cardiac difficulties aggravated by years of hard labor, the ear infection and deafness induced by torture, told us she was forty-four. It was Pat's forty-fourth birthday. "Different lives," she remarked. Pat, a boyishly handsome Washingtonian, tried to bridge the gap. "Same gray hair," he said.

The women's stories began to blend together, a parade of sick and mutilated people. At one point depression overcame the group. Silence, four people staring at the formica tabletop. One of us said something about there being people outside, in America, who knew she was here and would not forget her. Our institutions would remember. Several of the women wanted to make specific pleas, usually on behalf of nine prisoners purportedly confined in scattered places throughout Uruguay who had not been seen in more than a decade. We discussed the psychological pressure of incarceration, the food, the exercise or visitation privileges that guards often irrationally withheld. Often the lull of such normal prison conversation distracted me from empathy. Sometimes, when I remembered that many of these people had been imprisoned under ex post facto laws or for crimes of speech or association, my lawyerly sensibilities made me angry.

When I returned home to tell about our experiences in Punta Rieles, to write them up for our sponsors and a broader audience, I wanted to respond to the worries that we had before going, about being pawns in an Uruguayan propaganda show, about finding prisoners suspicious, about being unable to tell the true from the false in an environment that promised to be so foreign and exotic. I was repeatedly tempted to declare that the prisoners' stories

seemed by and large credible by all recognized indi-
cia of demeanor, but to make this judgment—to
enter into a debate about credibility—would also
have been to reduce and denigrate our experience at
the prison. To tell the truth about our time in Punta
Rieles seemed to require going beyond or outside assessments of credibility, out of reach of reason.

Of course this can be its own familiar tale, and
there is no doubt I also wanted to have been part of
the crude solidarity and witness that seemed so en-
dearing among the prisoners. At one point we heard
shouts from the cell block below us. Ana explained:
whenever anyone is removed from her cell, she yells
her number so that others can keep track of her and
know if she has disappeared. I want our visit to have
been like that. Sometimes, of course, it seemed so.
Ana wanted us to write down our names and the
names of our organizations so that she could tell the
others who it was who knew they were there. Print-
ing the names on a sheet torn from my notebook felt
great. In the face of such experiences of solidarity,
assessments of credibility did seem insignificant and
beside the point—you just had to be there.

But neither was our experience at Punta Rieles
simply one of solidarity and witness, however tempting it remains to flatten our time with the women into

a single unambiguous encounter, too true for de-
scription or proof in the worldly language we lawyers, so removed from grace, are used to speaking.
Moreover, refusing to analyze our prison experiences
in the language of credibility and doubt seems no
more faithful to Ana than doing so. Although it might
capture something of our solidarity with the women,
it would also suppress the ambiguities of our experience with them. They were also strategizing, emot-
ing, reciting scripts, and making it up as they went
along. In a way, assessing her credibility may be the
only way to avoid placing Ana on a pedestal of un-
touchable authenticity. Analyzing our experiences
from the remove of my Cambridge study, there seems
no escape from the simultaneous necessity and danger of assessing the truth of Ana's story.

One response to the difficulty of thinking truth-
fully "outside" the prison about an experience "inside" might be to acknowledge that the boundaries
which divide Cambridge and the prison, or which
separate my experiences from my analytical reflection, may be quite permeable. Perhaps we and they
were never so far apart, Uruguay never so foreign;
we never so innocent, so professional; they much
more than facts to be evaluated, victims to be avenged.
As I think about it, this permeability had some basis

in our experience. As we left the warden's office in
the other direction at 1:00 p.m., our prison visit con-
cluded, and returned to the gaze of the militia outside
the prison, the women hidden in one cell block were
singing "Happy Birthday." As the officers glanced
nervously at one another, we smiled at Pat.

6 ↟ CROSS-EXAMINATION: THE
    DOCTOR'S TALE

Both within and without the prison walls, our meetings with Uruguayan officials seemed purposive and
deliberative, lacking the easy give-and-take of our
meetings with the prisoners. As activists avenging
our prisoners' honor, we wanted our interactions
with Montevideo officials to be, first and foremost,
effective and official relations, and we embraced the
rhetorics of human rights and medical ethics enthusi-
astically. From the start, however, we had a hard time
finding the right mix of lawyerly aggression and
medical compassion with Uruguayan officials, and it
was difficult to release the full force of our concern
effectively.

We got our first chance to practice while still inside Punta Rieles. After speaking with the women

prisoners, we met with the prison doctor. He was a small and somewhat ugly bureaucrat, the perfect central-casting prison doctor. We had stalled him off all morning, brushing aside his offers to sit in on Richard's examinations, to spend time going over each medical record in detail—really, he kept repeating, to help us any way he could. Finally, as the last prisoner left, I asked him to come into the examining room. Richard was completing the notes of his medical examinations and skimming the prison medical files. Interrogation fell to me. After meeting with the prisoners and hearing their medical complaints, I wanted to cross-examine him to the wall. Two general problem areas seemed promising for interrogation: lack of patient confidentiality and the high incidence of torture-related complaints among the prisoners. After getting him to produce evidence confirming these charges, I would be able to force his acknowledgment of the newly adopted United Nations standards on participation by health workers in torture. I had a copy in Spanish and wanted to work through its terms with him.

I started with a setup question: could you describe your responsibilities at Punta Rieles? Your staff? Female doctors? Psychiatrists? Are they military officers? I figured I had about twenty minutes, including

translation. So far the facts looked good: the psychiatrists were military. In describing the range of medical complaints, the doctor emphasized an abnormal
incidence of psychological distress of various sorts,
spinal problems and other "functional" complaints
related to hypertension, and digestive irregularities.
Almost too good to be true for my case about torture.
I pressed on. We went through procedures for access
to medical care. I circled around, increased the pace
and had him on the run about patient trust. The
next step was confidentiality. Richard looked up and
slipped me the UN Code. One of his institutions had
been instrumental in drafting it, and he wanted to
make sure we spread the word. My time was short. I
switched to torture.

Did he know that charges had been made that the
Punta Rieles prisoners had been systematically tortured? Yes. By wrist suspension? Yes. What might be
the medical results of such treatment? I would need
to hurry. He couldn't speculate. Spinal dislocations?
My mind flashed to our forty-four-year-old and the
extra struggle ill prisoners confronted enduring the
Punta Rieles regime. I was furious with him for not
easing their burden. Suddenly everything was upside
down. The more he confirmed our worst suspicions,
the better my interrogation seemed. I pulled out the

UN Code. Did he know that international standards had been adopted governing medical personnel working in political prisons? He did. Did he know what they said? Yes. About torture rehabilitation? No. Had he seen this document? No commanding officer had ever put pressure on him to act unethically, he offered. I sensed a slip and restated the question: did he know what was required of medical officers regarding torture rehabilitation? Richard stepped in.

Surely the doctor sensed the importance of such standards for the profession as a whole, Richard soothed. Suddenly there were two doctors in the room. Solidarity. Mutual respect. He sprang for the escape. Yes, and he shared Richard's pride. It was an honorable calling. I was relieved but also frustrated. My anger had not yet found its outlet, although, as we reconstructed it later, the combination seemed defensible, both effective and authentic. Nonetheless, I was left hanging, enraged interrogator without a subject.

In part, confusion about the goals of our interrogation made our exchange with the prison doctor difficult. At times I could focus only on a desire to affect him, to imprint our visit on him one way or another— but why not just punch him out? Sometimes I wanted him to admit responsibility for Ana's suffering.

I wanted someone to blame and I wanted him to assume the role of the blameworthy and the stance of
subjugation before our witness to their deeds. At the
time, I did not worry that our interaction with the
doctor might lead him to treat his patients worse,
although with hindsight, I wonder why I did not.
Whether innocence or irresponsibility, it was easy in
those days to remain blind to such dark-side possibil-
ities. More often, we sought to induce the doctor to
change his ways, perhaps by getting him to recognize
a shared professional sense of the "reasonable" or
some external legal-ethical standard. We also thought
of being effective in ways that did not relate so directly to the object of our interrogation and, in particular, did not require him to change his behavior:
by bearing witness to his complicity, monitoring his
activity, expressing solidarity with his victims, and
reinforcing the human rights norms and institutions
with which we confronted him.

Sometimes these goals seemed to conflict or to
suggest divergent tactical mixes of lawyerlyness and
medical compassion. Getting the doctor to acknowledge a common professional norm seemed, at least to
Richard, to require tactics softer than those I was em-
ploying to force admission of his complicity and
show solidarity with his victims. Similarly, when I

thought we might best induce acceptance of a legal norm with a complacent tone, Richard hoped to bear witness with firmness. Nor could we face our sponsors if we seemed to have sold out. Even when we could resolve these dilemmas by imagining, as we did with the doctor, that our roles "complemented" one another, we often felt unsatisfied.

It is customary in the business to structure these ambiguities as personal choices between doing good and doing well. Thinking of things this way channeled my confusion and anger into a set of calculations manageably informed by my sense of my own moral agency. How, I asked, might I combine success and virtue, recognizing that neither authentic, human relations nor instrumental, effective encounters would alone be satisfying? After all, just as "effective" interrogation kept getting in the way of my relations with Ana, so a desire for "authentic" feelings, to express my anger, kept intruding on my talk with the doctor. By imagining that we wanted to be "effective without compromising our true beliefs," we could make authenticity seem like either a limit on being effective or a goal of secondary importance. I used this approach when one official described his pleasant days at Harvard. I considered whether to respond with a tone of common or divergent experiences in

tactical terms: how far could I go in appearing complicit before I would jeopardize his sense of our commitment to the prisoners? In the end, we traded a few
anecdotes about how Harvard Square had changed.

Once we started thinking this way, we were adept
at formulating strategies (one might even call them
doctrines) to accommodate our instrumental interest
and our moral position. Sometimes, for example,
we distinguished our reasonableness from the hard-
heartedness of our sponsors, or our professional reasonableness from the shocking facts of these particular cases. It was more difficult to arrive at a satisfying
resolution when our problem was a need to choose
either among conflicting moral values or among
conflicting tactics: how far, for example, might I
empathize with the prison doctor before denying my
sense of his injustice? Despite these strategic resolu-
tions, moreover, our confusion about goals never fully
disappeared.

To a certain extent, this fluid confusion served a
purpose. It often allowed us to differentiate our moral
and our instrumental selves, our retrospective sense
of the authenticity of our relations with the prisoners
and our more purely instrumental relations with
Uruguayan officials, without abandoning our sense
that these two dimensions of our personality and

activity were integrated in some way. Indeed, we pursued these official relations in part precisely to re-connect us with the authenticity we now imagined ourselves to have experienced with the prisoners.

As Richard asked the Punta Rieles doctor a series of questions about general health among the prison population, my mind turned to another doctor, on a podium in Paris four months before. As I had pushed through the crowd of leftists and luminaries gathered in the Assemblé Nationale for a conference on the Application of Humanitarian Law to the Conflict in El Salvador, an American physician was finishing his report on the health situation in the area of conflict. It was a numbing litany of statistics: birth weights, arm circumferences, and calorie counts. The crowd milled. I looked to see whom I might know in the hall. I wondered how this Manhattan internist had found his way to this motley conference, or to El Sal-vador for that matter. Probably some UNESCO tour. As his account came to a close, he concentrated on a family he had interviewed in the hills—a woman with four children, husband presumed dead or at war. The imagery is strong, of shrinking babies and sagging breasts, and the dirty faces of sickly children. He has the audience. Disease gives way to a rhythmic incantation of pharmaceutical shortfalls. Wounds that cannot be sutured, sores that cannot be salved. He knows we share his shame, his outrage, his intensity. He has taken us to El Salvador with him. He entreats us to make this conference a success, to respond to the wounds to which he is witness, to find—he pauses for breath before the climax—and to declare a right to health within the annals of humanitarian law. Applause. He is coming down, wiping sweat from his hands. We will respond; the lacuna in the law will be filled. He will not have gone, and we shall not have come, in vain. Two extra words have crept into his medical diction, promising to transport our concerns to the sick and the needy. Not health, but a *right to* health. Not engagement, but declaration.

After we had left the Punta Rieles doctor behind, I wondered how I, trying to release my emotions through the rhetoric of medical ethics or the device of cross-examination, differed from my Paris doctor, titillating us with barbarism while promising a successful, if disengaged, response. For my strategic planning and my tactics, like his, had been constructed to revive images of prisoners bound, and to bring our unresolved and often voyeuristic feelings about being with Ana and others safely into our normal lives.

Sitting with officials, we tended not to think about this. We were with them, after all, precisely because

we had left the prisoners firmly behind. If we did
wonder, as we projected as much self-assurance about
the naturalness of our presence as we could muster,
we did so in the language of standing: what right had
we to be there, asking these questions? Why should
the Punta Rieles prison open its files to us? The issue
of standing—the question of our right to intervene
in Uruguayan affairs—seemed to trouble the Uruguayans less than it bothered me.

What were we doing there? Increasingly, I see
worry about standing—like so many of the human
rights movement's self-flagellating debates: about
cultural imperialism, about "Asian values," about intervention and relativism and all the rest—as symp-
toms of our unwillingness to own a politics. And the
divided selves that go with politics, the intensity, the
desire, the will to power and submission, to affirm
and deny, to affiliate and disaffiliate.

I worried about standing when I perceived our relations with the Uruguayan officials in instrumental
rather than personal or human terms. But were there
other terms? The language of standing sprang up to
assuage our otherwise unresolved discomfort about
the chasm we were opening between our moral and
our professional selves. The instrumental intermed-
dler needs a basis for his intermeddlery. He needs a

doctrine like standing. But so does the anthropologist, the novelist, the photographer. We worried about standing to deny that our relations with the Uruguay- ans had a personal and human dimension. But did they? My experience with the doctor and the other officials was neither impersonal ritual nor human connection—any more than "becoming friends" with Richard and Pat. They were all complex social and personal crossroads in which dozens of desires, emotions, and roles found expression. Then, there- after, now. Perhaps I worried about standing simply to deny that I was brought there by an offscreen bar- barity, and I shared a secret desire to take one more look at the wound.

7 ⚉ THE MEN OF LIBERTAD

Back in the blue Peugeot, we speed to Libertad, prison for male politicos. The car is hot. Food and five minutes to relax with one another would be fine. If it weren't for the driver and the guide we could use this time to go over our Punta experiences, knitting them into sense. Behind schedule, we sit silently in the backseat, trying to turn our minds to the lon- ger list of male prisoners awaiting us. I close my eyes.

Libertad prison is in the countryside on the other side of Montevideo, in another military district. We see the massive rectangular building long before the sign reading "Rehabilitation Center #2." Just outside the inner grounds, in the military recreation area, healthy young soldiers are playing handball. In a cruel joke on parents who drive this road for brief telephone contact with their children, the last government bill-board before the prison depicts a small boy and girl, beside them the words "our hope." As we approach, I notice more uniforms, more checkpoints, more serious expressions, more guns.

There is no rite of passage into the prison here. Indeed, we never make it to the prison proper. As we step from the car, I can't make out the outline of the prison itself, obscured by too many watchtowers and outbuildings. Someone hands me a red identification badge as we step from the car, surrounded by gun-toting soldiers on a hardscrabble parking area. We trot between two walkie-talkie soldiers across a com-pound toward a small brick building. We step through the side door into an office labeled "Director." In-side, an officer in well-worn fatigues confronts us. There are no portraits here. On the walls are blurred black-and-white photographs of mangled bodies, victims of the Tupamaro terrorists.

59

The officer seems ill at ease with an international delegation. He plays it tough and close. State your business. We offer no elaborate introduction. Still standing, Richard hands him our list of names. We may see the three medical students. As to the other ill prisoners, that will not be possible. His orders from Montevideo include only three names. Our list lies limp on the table.

I assure him that this must be a misunderstanding. I suggest that we will gladly wait in his office while he straightens it out. No, he says, we will see the students now. In the meantime he will check with his commanding officer. This seems unlikely to clear anything up—the communications gap must lie between our political contacts in Montevideo and his superior, the commander for this military district. I think Papillon would have said that he would like to help us, if only . . . A truly malevolent director might have relished the rejection. This guy simply hands his list to someone and opens the door.

Guards take us to the visiting rooms. One wing of this outbuilding is partitioned into small chambers by walls of steel and glass. Inside each chamber are fifteen or twenty visiting posts—each with a telephone. Around the outside walls are phones for the prisoners. The wing is empty. The atmosphere beneath the

bare bulbs is tense. Our voices echo as we protest the
unacceptability of such a location for a medial exam. I
invoke medical confidentiality: Richard cannot examine a patient under such exposed conditions. Although
we will be able to speak privately with the students
within one visiting chamber, the glass walls are lined
with open telephones. There must be another room.
No dice. We are being neither let in nor kept out. I
can't seem to build a relationship with these men;
there are too many of them, they all look alike. Everything is moving too quickly; we can't sort out who
is who. We confer briefly and decide to go ahead on
their terms, more resignation than strategic bargain-
ing concession. Still, we hope our acquiescence will
advance our attempt to see the ill prisoners. We are to
have about twenty minutes with each student.

A steel door opens behind us, and through the
glass I can see a young prisoner being brought across
a barren field into the building. Head bowed and
shaven, he stands with his hands clasped behind him,
facing away from the guards who escort him. In a
gray uniform, number stenciled across his chest, he is
the image of subjugation. He catches my eye and
winks while the guards slide the door closed.

Ramon Hernandez shakes my hand. His eyes
brighten, and I realize that he may not have touched

61

someone from the outside since last June. As Pat races through our introduction, I notice new running shoes beneath his drab overalls. He is Ana's boyfriend. We convey her greetings. We admit there is nothing in particular that we want him to tell us, nor that we have to tell him. We are here, we explain, to see that he is all right and to be with him for the few minutes available.

Ramon puts our visit in political context: our presence here, he reasons, is an opening, a sign of the democratization process; the more significant when viewed in light of the recent release of two well-known political prisoners. He has heard of their release from a comrade who spoke with the Red Cross. We add as an afterthought that Richard will be glad to discuss any medical concerns Ramon may have. He nods. Ramon's political analysis has brought us together, no longer doctor-patient, lawyer-client, but four whisperers, talking politics. There are no artificial boundaries here, it seems, no artificially imposed violence, no hidden mysteries.

Ramon seems to know that he is supposed to tell his story, the story of his arrest and imprisonment. He tells it as though he were in a film: prisoner is brought to meet foreign delegation, describes prison conditions, tells some gory bits, seems in good spirits,

complains about the food; scene change. I enter his
script and take some ritualistic notes. He warms to
his subject. After his arrest, Ramon was charged with
membership in the student council of the medical
school, a charge he admitted in a declaration signed
after torture. He was beaten, doused with cold water,
forced to stand with his arms spread, deprived of
sleep, and hung by his wrists, tied behind his back.
He demonstrates each position with quick gestures. I
notice that he stutters. He touches his eyes, lips, ears,
and nose where the electric prod was applied. Also
his toes and genitals. Sitting cramped on a wooden
bench in this drab chamber, I picture him being tortured, his face smashed against the cement floor. The
police sanctum in which Ana had been violated had
seemed distant from the Punta Rieles clinic. Although we had been admitted to the prison, the site
of the violence had receded into mystery. Ramon's
story seems more violent, his environment tougher,
less subtle. He seems to have used his body, deployed
it, spent it. He is also an activist. By contrast, Ana's
pain seems extra, gratuitous, imposed. They tied
Ramon to an iron bed and attached electrodes to his
extremities and penis. He could hear the generator
too. I find myself recording the details in shorthand,
hiding the references in my notebook. My emotional

resistance has diminished. I feel as if I understand what has happened to Ramon.

Francisco Zelaya told a similar story, focusing slightly more on the details of time and place than had Ramon: eighteen hours of standing, two hours electricity, nine hours suspended by his wrists, etc. There had been a radio playing at the locations of his torture. Francisco is an animated boy; his eyes joke with us. We are all at a dinner party and he is describing the antics of an opposing soccer squad. I try to picture him with hair. The posters and documents they found in his apartment, he tells us, he had received unsolicited in the mail and never distributed. I think about the similarity of all alibis, the world round.

Libertad is a harsh regime: strict discipline, silence, poor food, infrequent visits. But Francisco seems in good spirits. He thinks medical treatment in the military hospital is fine, but complains about routine health care: waiting days for aspirin, and the like. His problems begin to sound trivial. He seems just another tortured youth, giving what he had in a battle with many fronts. Libertad's main terror seems to be punishment cells. Prisoners apparently begin their stay in these single unheated cells some distance from the main prison. There, without water, toilet facilities, or furniture beyond a bucket and mattress brought in at night, newcomers learn what can happen at Libertad. Francisco spent eleven days there. As he tells it, the worst seems stripped of mystery. I don't think it could happen to me, and, I suspect, neither does Francisco. Our connection has reaffirmed the gulf between us.

Victor Guerra, our last medical student, was different from the others. A veterinarian graduate, he seemed a naive and sensitive man. Where Ramon and Francisco had focused on the political context of our visit and told of their torture rather matter-of-factly, Victor seems more interested in pleading his defense, more embarrassed to be seen. He describes his arrest and initial appearance before a judge, explaining plaintively that the charges were exaggerated, the process defective. I am not a Communist. His soft eyes melt. Sheepishly, he describes his only political acts: attending a rally, voting against the military in a recent referendum.

Victor reengages me, in his case and in our mission. He explains that the whole group of medical students arrested the preceding June has yet to be sentenced. As I tumble to the fact that none of our students has been either tried or sentenced, hope returns that his incarceration and our visit might be creatively linked. Gone is the mutually resigned solidarity of our conversations with Ramon and Francisco.

Ramon and Francisco seemed to carry themselves as temporarily defeated warriors in a greater political struggle, and that is how they seemed to view their own stories of capture, torture, and imprisonment. Imprisoned warriors like Ramon and Francisco seemed our equals; they needed no rescue. To them we were comrades, coparticipants in a political struggle. The connection we had felt when in their presence—achieved by contrast with our experiences at Punta Rieles—diminished my sense of purpose. Like Ana, Victor, the passive victim, awakens my indignation and motivates me to act. Suddenly, our meeting the next morning at the court might be more than a formal plea for pardon. We might be able to do something. Victor, pleading legal procedure and propriety, rekindles our involvement, somewhat dampened by our abstract political solidarity with his fellows.

Victor describes his torture as if to convince us that it has really happened to him, telling against doubt and strangeness. If Ramon and Francisco spoke of torture ritualistically—three hours, two blows, 150 volts—Victor's pain comes through plainly as he details the familiar mix of blows, shocks, and other

tortures. Victor, a man without politics, suffers under
the harsh prison regime. As the guard returns for
him, he resumes the stance of subjugation, back to
his captor, head bowed, hands behind his back. He
cocks his head toward me and says softly in English,
"The position."

The three interviews have gone quickly. We are
exhausted and drained and have learned nothing new
about prison health care or about their legal cases.
We seem to have forgotten about being a delegation.
These interviews, each emotionally charged—the
wink, the touch, the words, the eyes—have disinte-
grated our difference, our special team spirit, and
made me feel subject, for the first time, to the Uruguayan regime. When Pat slips Francisco a cough
drop, it seems both natural and furtive, pressed by
the prison atmosphere. We glance apprehensively at
the guards walking on the other side of the glass. We
hear them talking down the hall. No flirtation here. I
compose myself. As we walk back to the director's
office, I straighten my posture and, somewhat fool-
ishly I think, try to look severe.

We were not to see the other prisoners. In part,
I was relieved. I wanted out. But I was also angry
and wanted revenge. Victor's parting comment had
unhinged me somewhat. Richard began a firm but

respectful dialogue with a junior officer. Snapped back into our delegation, we regained possession of the tools of anger and revenge, deployable emotions. We huddled in the hall to talk tactics. I wanted the director to feel threatened with responsibility for the failure of our mission if we were kept from seeing the ill prisoners. Richard thought the main players were in Montevideo, and that anger was likely to be wasted here. Besides, he was satisfied with what we had done. He suspected that the institutions would think it sufficient. I insisted. Faced with a malevolent opponent, I argued, we must be especially careful to see the one thing hidden from us: there will be secreted the smoking gun. Very lawyerly. Richard was unimpressed. Back in the office a second time, I expressed anger. Richard expressed disappointment. Pat mediated. We walked briskly to the car and left for Montevideo. It was 6:20 p.m.

8 ⚜ TRANSITION: PREPARING TO ACT

As I sat in the car on the way back to Montevideo, my mind turned eagerly to the tasks ahead. Unlike the drive from Punta Rieles to Libertad, this trip was animated. We had come out. Discussing what we were

to do in the coming days, we talked a bit too insis-
tently, too loudly, anxious to ignore the heat and
dust. In a way, we wanted to forget the prison, and I
was struck by the strength of my desire to put it behind us, to break forward from it, as if the memory
were pornographic. Just as the temptation in writing
about our prison experience with Ana was to analyze
the moment's ambiguity into recognizable patterns,
responsive to preexisting doubts, so driving back to
the city was itself a plunge forward into meaningful
action, and the temptation, for us then and or me
now, is to get on with the story of our Montevideo
follow-up. First, however, I want to suspend this
flight briefly to explore the ways in which the rush
to move from one place to the other helped to create
a system of images ordering the progress of our
mission.

Driving back to Montevideo, we differentiated
our time inside the prisons from activism outside
their walls in a couple of different ways. We felt the
intensity of "the moments we're all in this business
for," as a fellow human rights junketeer termed them,
those times when you seem able to see it like it really
is and in the face of which all else can be merely preparation or follow-up. This sense of difference makes
it seem only natural that activists returning from

adventures tend to think wistfully of their time away.
There was clarity and action—all the rest is com-
mentary. At the same time, we thought that our prison
visits needed—in fact, demanded—expression and
completion. Despite their apparent authenticity, as
the products of our preparation or the origin of our
response they seemed hollow. Suffering seemed
meaningful only when rendered productive. What
had been ambiguous or incomprehensible in the prisons would be clarified by our interpretive action in
response. Of these two differences, the second was
more useful, motivating the response we felt able to
give. For all these differences, however, the compli-
cated play of identities, roles, and names that had
characterized our relations with the warden and the
prisoners, as well as with one another, would be in-
tensified rather than set aside in Montevideo.

The mystery is that we experienced the drive not
as an active analytic process but as a natural transition from the country to the city. I am surprised,
thinking back, by the extent to which we sustained
this sense of spatial and temporal difference by rely-
ing upon notions about gender, distinguishing a
sphere of violation to be witnessed from a field for
active response. In prison we had been with the
women, the victims, and we were returning to the

men, victimizers in Montevideo. It would be enough simply to repeat what we had heard. A woman was tortured. Electrodes on her genitals. Female victims, profane men—and male avengers. In this frame, we would represent Ana far more than Ramon, Francisco, or Victor. Maybe once electrodes had been placed on their genitals, they were women. It was hard to think of them as either engaged, fighting, deploying themselves, or as suffering. Suffering as men.

In Montevideo, we felt, it would all be on our will, our reason, our action, to avenge and expiate what we had experienced. It was grandiose thinking, inflated by the effort to think ourselves different, from the prisoners, the prisons, from the whole place. We had kept our relations with Papillon purposive and fluid by holding before us the promise of access to Ana. Coming out, these contrasts made us feel we were back on familiar ground, activists with a cause. All these differences helped us feel we were moving, first toward, then away from, on behalf of the prisoners. Together, they structured our sense of progress, of moving meaningfully forward with our mission. They gave us the feeling of simultaneous engagement and distance, of having touched the forbidden and of being able to respond to it, recasting the violence we had heard about in the vocabulary of calculation and barbarism with which we had prepared our visit, and which we would use to complete it. Both inside the prison and en route to Montevideo, the violation of women's bodies kept something hidden and mysterious, so that something else, intentional knightly deployment, could seem familiar.

At the same time, my sense of connection with the male prisoners was achieved by contrast with our experiences at Punta Rieles. Once we had reimagined Ana's torture as an abomination, forgetting our elaborate efforts to connect with her as a person, a political sympatico, it became possible to relate more objectively to Ramon's tales. Ramon seemed subjugated, not violated. His pain was instrumental, his body political. Ana had been trespassed upon, Ramon punished. We repeated this contrast within Libertad between Ramon-Francisco and Victor, the victim. Thinking about it later, I realized we had also imagined our forty-four-year-old as a spent warrior, different from Ana.

In rethinking the trip, I am struck by our repeated effort to transform an experience—talking with Ana—into something more directional, purposive. Not just experience, but *action*, going, returning, avenging, engaging, and so on. In an odd sense, the entire project was less about crossing boundaries than it was about sharpening the distinctions that could transform experience into action. There and then we had experienced; here and now we would act. Keeping this going kept alive, may even have deepened, the distinctions between Uruguay and "the international community," between the victims and the abusers, the men and the women, the innocent and the politically engaged. The odd thing is that we did not think of this as interpretation— indeed, we experienced only a rush to move on with the show.

Thursday evening, back in Montevideo after a day at the prisons, we sat around a quiet table at a bar near our hotel, reveling in our success, and strategizing our remaining thirty-six hours in the country. Getting into the Uruguayan prisons burdened us. We wanted to maximize our positive impact, paying our debts and finishing what we had started. As we headed out, the pace of the trip quickened dramatically. The next day we were to appear before the chief judge of the Supreme Military Judicial Court to plead for the early release of the prisoners who had become subjects of our concern. There were meetings with families, human rights groups, political parties, and government officials. We would return

to the United States Embassy to brief rather than to
be briefed. There were press releases, reports, and
law review articles to be written. We had to confirm
our onward flight to Santiago, where we would begin
again. More prisons, more activists—and a visit with
my graduate school roommate, now a Connecticut
banker in Pinochet's Chile.

It may have been wishful thinking or tired excitement, but by Thursday afternoon we suspected that
the hearing at the Supreme Military Judicial Court
set for Friday morning might be more than a formality. Government moderates had surprised us by
hinting that our four students might be released after
our visit. Perhaps contending government factions
had struck a deal, and our visit would be the occa-
sion for a demonstration of largesse. Procedurally,
we had discovered that no judgment had been en-
tered. It would not be too late to drop the charges.
The sentences, due in three weeks, might at least be
reduced to time served. I began to hope that our pre-
sentation, if done right, might increase the likeli-
hood of such an outcome. At the very least, I didn't
want to jeopardize a deal, should one have been
struck, and I had professional pride in presenting a
good oral argument.

But should I be easygoing or formal? Present myself as an attorney pleading four cases or as a humanitarian interloper representing five North American institutions? Should I plead our clients' naïveté? Rehabilitation? Minimizing the chances of error if a deal had been struck seemed to require more role fidelity and formality—a more ritualistic pre-sentation, a greater emphasis on official Uruguay— than did effective adversarial advocacy. More than just tactical choices, these seemed to pose a conflict between honest witness and ceremonial advocacy. Was it time to come out of the closet, or should we wait until we left Montevideo? Until our prisoners were finally released?

In all these scenarios, invoking international law seemed the least promising strategy, in part because the court would need to repudiate a good bit of its autonomous and legal self-image to find international law relevant. Nevertheless, I thought that mention-ing international law might in some fuzzy way strengthen international norms. More important, this approach seemed most closely connected to any the-ory of our standing (and my competence) that I could devise. Perhaps, I theorized, once a state violates a widely accepted norm of human rights, it loses the right to oppose jurisdictional interference, if not legally, at least in terms of perceived cultural and political legitimacy. This exchange theory seemed comforting, for it grounded our presence in their conduct, if not their direct consent.

In the end, however, I decided to abandon international law and not to worry about standing. If they had any objection to my appearance, I would try to answer it on other grounds, perhaps agreeing to argue on general humanitarian terms if the judge would hear no argument on the specific cases. In retrospect, this shift from a formal standing doctrine to one based in humanitarianism seems fragile. At the time, however, I felt I was escaping doctrine for the bravado of a more direct advocacy style. In any case, having abandoned legalism, I suddenly became obsessed with the idea that I needed more information about the court, the judges, the law, the advocacy practices, the local cultural norms of humanitarianism. In short, about Uruguay.

Thursday evening, Pat and I phoned everyone we could think of to set up meetings with attorneys who had represented prisoners before Judge Ledesma. We came up with three, including the attorney of record for one of our students, and arranged appointments for Thursday night and Friday at breakfast.

I sat down at an old portable typewriter to draft a press release and oral argument for the next morning. Afterward, we taxied from lawyer to lawyer to pin down the details of Uruguayan military court procedure and test-run my evolving argument.

In a nicely appointed apartment twenty minutes outside Montevideo, we found the attorney for one of our students. She was a thin, upright woman in her middle fifties who had been representing these "youngsters" for several years. As she spoke, my burgeoning hope for the following day shrank. Yes, she condescended, the fact that the judge would hear us might mean something. Anything might mean something. But I should realize, she stressed as I questioned her about the court's jurisdiction and procedure, that these were not trials but the imitation of trials. She was cynical about newfangled human rights concerns. Where had the political parties been, and where, for that matter, had we been, during the long Uruguayan political silence? She had been driving to the prisons to seek access to her clients, supporting their families, filing habeas corpus petitions as witness to their incarceration. To represent these prisoners had nothing to do with their release, or with sentence reduction. To represent them was not to forget them when nothing could be done.

She addressed me in English. She had seen no files, had not been permitted to discuss the charges with her clients, had been interrogated and searched upon reaching the prisons. To have challenged the court's procedure would have been to risk professional sanction. At my insistence she outlined the typical case history—arrest, summary process, first instance, decision, sentence, review—in a distracted and distant manner. Here, in her middle-class sitting room, sitting stiffly forward in her chair, she described the paperwork of prosecution and defense abstractly, without meeting my gaze, as if she were describing some embarrassing, though fortunately distant, family scandal. But for all her distance, I felt she was teasing us, holding out the promise of something, something beyond cynicism. We were not like her, not Uruguayan, yet she kept hinting, if only we asked the right question, showed the right solidarity, she would release her secret.

Finally, I asked her what she, a lawyer, would do if, like me, she were to face Judge Ledesma ten hours later. Colonel Ledesma, she corrected me, adding somewhat incongruously that I should "not challenge his assertions about procedure and about the court's fealty to law." He will say he can do nothing: that the case is not yet before him; that military law is punctilious about procedural regularity. She scoffed. Stress, she advised, that these are young prisoners, awkward victims of tough political times, without records, who were picked up for pursuing the natural student curiosity about ideas. I wondered whether this story bore any relation to the cases. She didn't know, not having yet been able to see their files. A factual plea for mercy on fabricated facts seemed risky to me. Yet as she settled on this course, she warmed to our inquiries.

This was a technical, professional problem; fashioning an oral argument. She gave it her best shot, and as our adrenaline began to flow in the hopeless late-night aura we found professional solidarity. Nevertheless, as we left her on her porch at 12:30 a.m., I felt a bit foolish for having imagined there to be any point to my efforts in Uruguay other than the working out of professional courtesies. Yet for all her tragic demeanor, before we left she took my notepad for a moment and, in a rigid block script, printed the names of the three other clients. Gonzalo Mujica Benoit, five years, six months; Ricardo Cohen Pappo, twelve years; Dr. Guillermo Dermit Barbato, five years. Like others whose names would be pressed upon us in the coming hours, these, too, had a "medical angle," had suffered, deserved our attention.

9 ⚚ A MOMENT OF ADVOCACY

At 9:00 the next morning, the Peugeot dropped us at
a modest building of stone, identified only by the
most discreet chiseling beside the door: Supreme
Military Judicial Court. The door opened onto the
tiled entrance court of a nineteenth-century city villa.
We were ushered up a lavish central oak staircase
beneath a stained-glass skylight. In and off the
courtyard sat military clerks and guards. Around the
second-floor lobby were the judicial offices. One,
crammed with files on open shelves, showed the only
sign of business. I felt the European aristocracy de-
based, their court, still noble in service of a democracy, overrun by the philistines. To the left, an ornate
office—head of the Supreme Court—brocade,
leather, oak, and books reduced to signs of the law,
and of the tradition.

A large man with an open collar approaches us.
Car salesman turned judge. His very severe aide introduces him. She, her mouth a penciled formality
beneath rouge cheeks, will translate. I thank her,
but we have brought our own. Although we know
Ledesma speaks English, the rituals of power and respect have taken over. The aide ushers us in. Four
chairs have been arranged before his desk, three

upright black, one of elaborate red brocade. As we shuffle around the room, I sit decisively in the red chair, perhaps only to befuddle our would-be translator. Ledesma, after some hesitation, produces a second red chair from behind his desk and sits.

Richard introduces us, politely, firmly, and presents thick written appeals from our five sponsoring organizations. I am grateful for word processing. Ledesma interrupts. As this is legal business, and he is a lawyer, he will deal directly with the lawyer. Lawyer to lawyer in a court of law. The word *law* festoons his every phase. The Spanish word for lawyer sounds like "avocado." The avocado will speak.

I speak slowly, in a tone that I hope will secure ten minutes without interruption. The translation pauses heighten the drama. Phrase by phrase. I don't want to impinge upon these prisoners' proper defense, nor prejudice their legal claims, nor interject any inappropriate considerations into his formal and legal deliberations. I want to speak to him only as one lawyer to another. I think: What does this mean? Why would we be here if not to introduce pressure beyond military law? He nods and seems satisfied. We have given a sign that we will stay within the protocol assumptions about his dignity as an independent judicial officer. He will reciprocate.

We have come, I intone, to appeal for the earliest possible release of four medical students arrested last summer on charges of subversive association. I have not had access to their files and cannot speak as their counsel, but I speak on behalf of the many thousands of American scientists who have been concerned about these students. Of course, we seek no special treatment for medical prisoners, or for these individuals, beyond what the law allows. The contradictions mount. This appeal is grounded in general considerations, considerations of international concern, international law, and political democratization that apply to other cases, to be sure. But it is also an appeal specific to these individuals. With his permission, I would like to go over these specific cases. He nods. I am glad I have remembered my opening set of points. The tone seems OK. The sergeant-translator looks uneasy. I proceed.

I portray our students as naive children, refer to our visit with them, itself an important signal of Uruguay's political openness. I describe their eyes. Their offenses are nonviolent, crimes of curiosity. They renounce violence; their punishment has already been severe. I do not mention how hard it is for the international community to comprehend such punishment for crimes of association: for Uruguay's friends

to hear of physical abuses that contravene international obligations. Perhaps this omission is a mistake.
He breaks in.

The judiciary is independent and will follow the
law. Why does he keep saying this? He delivers an
elaborate discourse on the independence and procedural formality of the military judiciary, a speech
oddly incongruous with his availability to hear an ex-
traordinary appeal from five U.S. scientific institutions before the trial court has even convicted our
medical students. Superfluous protestation. But he is
just warming up. These are dangerous, violent criminals with years of hardening political experience.
Can that be right? Although he is merely repeating
Papillon's story, it throws me off momentarily, feeds
directly my doubts about my standing, my oral strategy. I say nothing. I am reassured to remember that a
judge is not supposed to deliver, before conviction, a
speech one might expect of a warden.

The country is in danger. Families have lost members to political violence. He can never forget that.
His contradictions mount. He, of course, can't comment on specific cases. He pulls four files from his
desk. Which was the veterinarian? Victor Guerra.
These individuals have been involved in ten years of
political work. Work that was, I think, but do not say,

legal at the time. He will of course, review these cases when he receives their files. He will certainly take what we have said into account. Despite his legal demeanor, he seems unaware of such basics of legal protocol as no ex post facto laws, individual guilt and innocence, no associational crimes, innocent until proven guilty, and judicial restraint in discussing cases before the court.

Our presence poses a classic dilemma for him. He must defend his regime, yet any defense will derogate from the propriety that is his best defense. I am also in a bind. Once in his court, I must speak to Ledesma's self-image, yet to do so betrays the ground of our presence. We are each insecure about the ground for the meeting, and as contemptuous of the other's naïveté about the law as of our own gullibility. We embrace the lawyer's role and language to speak in contradiction, but are cynical about it. Polite, respectful, and cynical. It is even a cynicism we can share in a chortle about the protocol of the chairs.

As he stands up, signaling our imminent departure, I begin to suspect that something lurks beneath this cynicism, some rage or fear or tactic that sustains and justifies the pretensions. I think if only I can keep going, it will emerge. But the audience, a formal success, in which we have seemed reasonable, articulate, and firm, is over. Although I am glad that I haven't blown it, I measure my performance against this hidden image. Having not thrown off my role, having not really spoken my heart, I feel I have failed to touch him. He has neither admitted complicity nor told me what he really thinks. Ledesma relaxes and points to a chair in the corner of his office, the one-time possession of an Uruguayan Founding Father. He exclaims proudly, with a sweeping gesture, that the tradition ends here, in this office. We descend the stairs, Ledesma behind us. Clerks snap straight. Heels click. Doors swing open and we step into a waiting car. As we pull from the curb, Ledesma smiles broadly, waving until we have pulled around the corner, out of his sight.

10 ⚵ THE AFTERMATH

We spent our remaining twenty-four hours in Uruguay with human rights groups, political party members, the press, and with the relatives of the disappeared, of political prisoners, of our medical students, and of victims of Argentinean repression. We tried to be supportive and to share our experience, that we might release our emotions of solidarity and frustration, and, perhaps, that they might be released from isolation. We tried to be informal and empathetic, without breaking the confidence of our prisoners and government contacts. Sometimes we connected, but, I fear, more often we failed.

Those with whom we spoke often seemed to refuse emotional connection with us, transforming us into something foreign and exotic, the responsible and incapable. Why, they sometimes asked, had we chosen these prisoners when others, their lovers, sons, and mothers, had suffered so much more? Often, on the other hand, they were respectful, treating us as foreign professionals, from whom nothing personal could be expected. We won gratitude more often for our official than for our personal presence. They thanked us as the representatives of our institutions, and the thanks seemed heartfelt.

Some of those we met seemed politically informed and able to locate our visit quite concretely in their stories about social conflict and suffering in Uruguay. Others seemed bewildered by their situation, by our presence. The mother of one prisoner seemed to have been plucked from her middle-class bridge game and plunked down amid young radicals, press oppositionists, and now foreign delegations, fully without preparation or premeditation. As we managed the flow of one delegation after another through our hotel bar on Friday afternoon, we moved in and out of our professional roles and changed the level of political neutrality we projected. Sometimes we struck a formal pose, hoping that its improbable rigidity would signal our true sympathy. I remember declaiming quite piously to a sympathetic young journalist and his microphone, when asked to comment on upcoming Uruguayan elections, that "our concern has been with public health, not public policy." He nodded, and I thought he understood what I felt and why I did not say it.

There seemed no way to share the facts of our prison visits with the students' parents. They wanted to know too much and could hear too little. At one point, wrapped in my best demeanor of foreign authority, I assured some mothers solemnly that "yours are children to be proud of." It's what I tell parents at the Harvard graduation lunch. We seemed to connect. At times the tangle of expectations rankled. As Richard set me up to interview one group about their legal cases because he thought they would feel better, tempers flared. By 11:00 p.m., sitting down to dinner, the three of us needed to release the day's tension.

At a gaudy restaurant around the corner from our hotel we found ourselves laughing giddily, imitating ourselves promising, cajoling, reassuring. We slept well.

Rituals. We talked again to U.S. officials at the Montevideo embassy. One man described such engagement as the U.S. government has with the Uruguayan military around human rights issues this way: "We do what we can, send them up to Panama, and tell them about constitutions and so forth, but it doesn't seem to stick." As if the Uruguayans had not simply learned something else from their American sponsors, something about running a military prison. But we knew what he meant, or why he said it, and I was glad when he put the rest of our talk off the record. We, like they, had heard it all before.

Although there was nothing in what we reported that had not been repeatedly documented, as we spoke about torture in Uruguay there was a sense in which these embassy political and human rights officers seemed to be hearing about it for the first time. They were hearing it from Americans, we who had crossed to the other side, and they could hear it anew. Still, just as we, in talking with the prisoners, had oscillated between a nauseous fascination and a vacant sense of ennui, so these officials seemed both fascinated and

bored by our story. It all seemed so familiar, so jad-
ing, so tragic.

At the end of a trip such as this, I have always felt
a little guilty. As I realize that I am leaving, returning
to my classes in Cambridge, I feel I am betraying
those I came to serve and that I won't be able to respond successfully or sufficiently to what I have seen.
As we packed our bags in Montevideo, these feelings
came over me quite strongly. I felt somehow corrupt,
as if we had deceived the Uruguayans for our own
professional and personal reasons. It seemed that the
true price of constituting Uruguay as at once foreign
and exotic was not to be paid in Montevideo, as I had
feared while leaving Boston. It was to be paid upon
my return, as I became once more foreign to them,
disconnected and out of touch. It seemed impossible
for a marginal American law professor to discharge
the obligations I felt to those we had met in Uruguay.
So many people had told us their stories, looked to us
for help, asked us to take on their struggle, to work
when we got back. Even those who understood the
limits of our context spoke with both resignation and
hope about "international public opinion" whose
symbol we three became, if only for an instant. We
kept saying that our institutions would "remain concerned," that we would write a report, that we would

carry their story back. But three individuals cannot fulfill the promise implicit in the words *foreign, American, professional, authority, witness*.

Despite these thoughts, as we drove along the beach out of town, I felt buoyant. I considered our latitude. With good fortune, this autumn sun would have brought spring to Boston by the time we returned. When we got back, we would continue the work we had come to do. For the moment, our work in Montevideo completed, we enjoyed the tourist paradise this coast must have been. I was glad Richard and Pat and I would be able to stay in touch when we got home and was thankful that we would be able to count on a network of human rights activists for institutional support. In a way, I was glad to find myself becoming a human rights professional. Perhaps I should teach a course, get more involved, do this again.

Coming to Uruguay, our identities as professionals and our affiliations with the institutional machinery of human rights protection had been reassuring. We had felt prepared. Patrick, armed with the analysis of political science, would be able to open up the complexities of a shifting social and cultural environment, taming the foreign power struggle. Richard, bringing the ethical conventions and special talents

of the medical profession, would be able to render
that most dispassionate of compassions, medical as-
sistance, rendering suffering as diagnosis, if not cure.
I had compiled the relevant treaties to which Uruguay was signatory and read up on military court
procedures. I hoped to provide a point of access, a
justification and normative basis for our involvement, orienting us to a right and wrong, permissible
and impermissible, where everything would be different. As we returned to our American identities,
we were again reassured by these points of connection. They promised us continued access to the land
we were escaping.

But medical, political, and legal science can only
partly redeem this promise. They provide continued
access to foreign situations in part because they seem
objective, neutral, scientific, above the differences
that divided us from Ana and Ramon, from the warden and the embassy. This dispassionate image
helped us feel connected to Uruguay in part by in-
stilling confidence that we could retain our difference
and distance. International human rights law reassured me that I could think of concrete moral out-
rages while remaining safely distant from them.

International human rights law is self-consciously
about foreign violence and distant human suffering.

Modern human rights advocacy was born in the desire to respond to nonmilitary atrocities that seemed
unthinkable, incomprehensible, even banal. It was
imagined into being by people who wanted to know
these atrocities, tame them, name them "genocide,"
bring them into polite parlance. Human rights activists struggled to develop a "right not to be tortured"
or a "right to health"; to reach out with empathy, as-
sistance, and protection to people who are tortured
and sick. They thought of their work as a response of
civilized society, the response of reason to that which
it cannot comprehend. They began a process of
treaty drafting and bureaucracy building that has
been carried on by subsequent enthusiasts, bureau-
crats, and politicians until one can speak confidently
of a "network" or "community" of international
human rights advocates and professionals.

But when we found ourselves in the field in Uruguay, it was not at all clear that the world came to us
neatly divided into reason and chaos. Looking back,
I see that it was far more our project to mark out this
distinction on an ambiguous terrain. As I think about
it now, I worry about the extent to which human
rights sustains the image of irrationality to which it
purports merely to respond. It was not realistic, in
fact, to dream as we drove along the beach that the

human rights movement could discharge the taint of distance from those we had come to know in the Uruguayan prisons. The human rights bureaucracy, built up so dramatically since we were in Uruguay, is as much the machinery of our mutual estrangement as of any connection. Not only because on the ground in Montevideo we kept marking sharp distinctions in soft sand to move ahead, to make our advocacy count. In the years since, we have also learned that torture is itself a legal regime, that torturers and politicians also play with words, mark boundaries, and strategize, often using the same words and the same stories.

I have repeatedly been surprised by the difficulty human rights lawyers have acknowledging that there is law on the other side. That when they invoke human rights against state power, human rights advocates are pounding not only on the door of politics, but also on sovereign privilege and constitutional right. In some way, for human rights, inhumanity must always remain distant, across a great divide. A violation, a barbarity, a lapse. The exception, the extraconstitutional, the deviation. Guantánamo a black hole in the fabric of law.

Torture was at the center of our trip, as it has been at the center of this story. And yet we worked constantly to locate the barbarism elsewhere—while we were still in Boston, we placed it in Uruguay; driving to the prison, we placed it behind the walls. Even with Ana, our interrogation tamed her story, placing her pain in the past at some distant police station. Leaving town, we left it all behind us. I remember discussing our mission, before I went, with a human rights bureaucrat friend of mine, who said, "Even if you don't get inside the prisons, you'll have struck a blow for human rights." My mission was, it seemed, independent of any actual contact with any actual torture. It required only that torture be out there. That torture be reported. As a human rights advocate, I relied far more upon the narrative unknowability of violence than on any mechanism for rendering it comprehensible, infiltrating its terms, or coming to grips with its logic.

In some way the professional practices of the human rights community embolden us precisely by reassuring us that we can know, can engage, and ultimately can control things we are also right to imagine as outside civilization and reason, foreign to our own lives. As human rights activists, we can touch the barbaric and return unscathed. As "lawyers" pursuing "remedies" for "abuses" of "human rights," we find a string of articulation joining our images of civilization and our understanding that many suffer in its hands. We find a way to acknowledge their suffering without abandoning our commitment to the system that produces it; indeed, we cast ourselves as those whose role will be its elimination. Torture and violence remain "out there," like the prisoner-victim, perceived only dimly, remembered by the metonymic invocation of the prisoner, the body, the victim. As a result, I'm afraid my dream of a human rights movement that could link us with all we had experienced remained a dream. Immersion in the machinery of international human rights could not discharge the taint of our distance from those we had come to know in the Uruguayan prisons, precisely because that bureaucracy is the machinery of our mutual estrangement as much as of any connection.

This was not visible to us in Montevideo. We thought it difficult at times for a doctor and a lawyer to relate to one another. We thought it was hard to understand what Ana had experienced, difficult to get her to tell her story. We wondered about our effectiveness. But we did not wonder whether we were contributing to the estrangement we felt in Ana's presence. We were too busy trying to do as well and as much as we could. We just did not have the time.

Common as this feeling may be, I suspect it is no longer so easy to avoid the tough questions. Human rights advocates and practitioners are no longer so naive, so innocent. The movement has grown up since we were in Uruguay, and modern human rights professionals are often the first to know and to admit the limits of their language, their institutional practices, their governance routines. They know there are darker sides; they weigh and balance and think shrewdly and practically. At the same time, the profession has developed routine practices to disperse the nausea and still the confusion we felt in Montevideo. They are careful to separate their public piety and their private cynicism, the pragmatism of the field and the earnestness of headquarters, the rhetoric of public relations and the reality of recruiting all those victims and gathering all that testimony, lest mixing the one with the other damage the endeavor or discourage the donors. As a result, knowledge of the dark side is as readily denied as admitted. In the field, it is denied in the name of the pragmatic, at headquarters in the name of ethical commitment.

For me, that week in the spring of 1985 was all about doubt and ambiguity and things we didn't know. As I have told about our time in Uruguay over the years, the story has come together in quite

different ways. In the glory days of human rights—
and in the report we filed with our sponsors on our
return—our meeting with Ana seemed the climax
of an adventure, North meets South, lawyer meets
client; come to the field to make abstract norms
real. Ana's tremble and Pat's soothing writer-doctor-
lawyer speech seemed to fix a point between two
worlds: native and foreign, authentic subject and objective role, the agents and their mission's object,
cultural or political life and the law. In the pressure
cooker of academic identity politics, the whole story
often seemed to be about my sexism. Torture, along
with self-consciousness, faded from view. In subsequent years, as the bloom came off the rose of human
rights, whenever I taught the story, our trip seemed
to foreshadow what many then were discovering
about the dark sides of human rights advocacy.

It has been through retelling experiences like this
one that human rights has become a profession—
that the movement has been sold to donors, has re-
cruited new talent, learned from its mistakes, and
developed a more professional sensibility about what
it undertakes. In the meantime, much that we worried about and didn't understand has been filled in by
professional expertise. There are research teams to
tell you about local court practice and who runs

which prison. Hundreds of grassroots organizations have been funded to support the work of the international human rights profession on the ground. Volumes have been written on strategy and best practice. All this telling and retelling has spawned a new pragmatism among human rights professionals. We remind one another to analyze, strategize, keep our powder dry, weigh and balance. We are confident we know a great deal about how human rights work, what makes advocacy effective and where the difficulties lie. The wisdom of the field has been harnessed to the commitments of headquarters, just as the broader perspective of the international leadership chastens the excessive enthusiasm of the local advocate or volunteer.

But I am convinced there remains something to learn from our earlier, more amateur uncertainty and unknowing. Not because we saw the dark sides more clearly or had better, more spontaneous ideas about what to do. But because we were puzzled by what we encountered, found it difficult to tell where light and dark lay, and could still see the work of narration necessary to transform all that we experienced into professional knowledge. Consequently, I have written it here less to underline all we have learned than to evoke again the amateur's sense of not knowing what things mean or where they are going in human rights work. I have told about our time with Ana less to figure out what finally happened than to remember how much we had to learn. To explore the ways our search for the right tactic produced results we could not evaluate, how our inability to know what was intrusive in a situation we had defined as foreign left us confused about our connections and responsibilities. So many efforts described as either noble and important or misguided and trivial continue to be experienced more directly as tawdry and uncertain. It is good to remember how that feels. Indeed, much that we have since learned about the dark sides of human rights *was* present from the start. But if we can see that now, at the time we experienced it more often as hesitation, uncertainty, or worry.

Thousands of pages have been written about international human rights in the years since I traveled to Montevideo. I remain struck by the narrow range of narration. So many of the stories we tell about human rights missions have a similar plot: a knight bursts forth from his domain, has a number of adventures crossing borders, foiling enemies, or bonding friendships, and eventually reaches the land beyond the pale, returning with tales aplenty. Bad actors are exposed, shamed. Victims are avenged. Or, later, the knight grows up and looks back with sad wisdom on what once seemed so daring, so bold. Societies compromise and heal, make the "transition" to justice. In the end, even the sagacity of the more experienced professional is also a story. The story of jaded and mature professionalism, of knowingness.

All these stories are important. They instruct. But they also reinforce ideas about potent actors and their terrain, placing the calculating activist, or the reflective elder, at center stage, bringing reason and justice to the land of the unjust, the victimized, and surviving to tell and untell the tale. It will be the storyteller who decides when to compromise, how to knit the social fabric, once rent by denunciation, back together as reconciliation. In these stories, we construct our action and the societies on whom we act in stereotypes, just as we do our own later, more chastened, wisdom. In all this, telling about a human rights mission and undertaking one are not as different as they sometimes seem. Both activities seek to transform the ambiguity and confusion of moments like ours with Ana into comprehensible narratives, whether triumphal or otherwise.

After Montevideo, out of the prison, as the moment marked by Patrick's words and Ana's behavior came to be acted upon and analyzed, his words took precedence over her suffering. And then my words replaced his. It is so difficult not to imagine time passing as a succession of burials, and beneath it all, her suffering. It is tempting, thinking this way. We may easily come to imagine that the way out lies in affirming that human rights takes place on a field of pain and death—that torture, bodies in pain, mute, confront and confound our efforts to make meaning. Were we to walk in their shoes, suffering marked on our bodies, we would not be puzzled by narration and legitimation. Mangled bodies lie now as always outside all that. At the same time, and I am afraid in equal measure, suffering confirms our story, grounds it, gives it direction, makes memory worth the struggle.

As a response to the limits of our habitual narratives, invoking the primacy of bodies in pain seems no more satisfying to me now than it did at the time. Ana neither confirms nor confounds. She is a story, at once more puzzling and mixed up than that. We simply do not have a route back, to the bottom, be it her suffering or Pat's words or even the strange alchemy by which the one conjured the other. What we have is a story, at times predictable, at times frustratingly unsteady. Our work then, Ana's and Victor's and Ledesma's no less than my own, than Pat's and Richard's, was narration. It is in that context that I hope our amateurish confusion might provide some kind of antidote to the routines of professional sensibility that have arisen in the ensuing years.

I hope that in those befuddled moments we might catch a glimpse of the elusive and heady experience of human freedom and of the weight which comes with the responsibility of moments like that. I know no better way to evoke this than to remember how strange it was to do human rights for the first time— Ana had never before been imprisoned nor interviewed by a foreign doctor, we were Papillon's first foreign delegation, and Richard, Pat, and I had never worked as a team. In those amateur days, you sometimes could feel the human experience of freedom and bear the weight of responsibility. Not responsibility enforced and judged in some later narrative, but the mysterious feeling of being free and responsible right now, of making it up for the first time.

As we drove along the beach on the way out of town, this was the last thing on our minds. We hoped that once we got home, the human rights movement would offer us a way both to continue and to end our experience in Uruguay. By turning it over to professionals, or by becoming professionals ourselves, we might strike a blow for human rights, while also finding a way to go on to other things. It would be, in the

end, simply our work. We could again imagine ourselves distinct from Uruguay; we could come and go,
relating through our roles as we crossed and recon-
stituted the barriers of estrangement. What had
seemed puzzling and distressing this time out would
become routine. We would need a bureaucracy and
a discourse of connection. We would need human
rights to take us there and bring us back, to reduce
the variety of our experience to rights and duties,
victims and perpetrators. Rights to eat, to work, to
develop, to live in peace, to be free from torture—
somewhat different from food, jobs, social change,
peace, release, but as close as we could come. As we
grew up with the movement, it was easy to forget
what we glimpsed in the confusion of Uruguay. Or
to remember it simply as the shameful naïveté of the
amateur.

Somewhere along the way, the human rights
movement also grew up and lost the appetite for political decision, for personal freedom of action and
the weight of human responsibility. It preferred the
smooth and knowing routines of professional advocacy, just as the three of us, leaving Montevideo,
hoped to settle comfortably into what was then just
an emerging discourse and profession. In the plane
to Santiago, we dictated a bit; as the plane prepared to

land, we got together and prepared for another round of the work we'd come to do. We would get better. The movement would become powerful. But somewhere deep down, even the most dedicated human rights professional knows that what can seem urgent and noble is often also tawdry and voyeuristic. Our ethics seems impractical, sentimental, inauthentic. At the same time, our pragmatism stains our piety. Still, I know that somewhere we also remember that it has all been a story, and that next time we could do something different.

EPILOGUE

February 11, 1985, Pat writes from Washington:

> Other than writing news, we've got a new baby girl, named Glenna. (By the way, in case Richard didn't mention it: Ramon Hernandez was released New Year's Eve. All the others were out in September. That gray haired woman who was only 44 was released in August.) And Silva Ledesma, when I saw him in November, to make yet one more pitch for

Ramon, was thinking about the future, remembered that I was an *escritor*, and wondered
whether perhaps I might be able to give him
some advice about New York publishers.
Seems he's been writing short stories. Ciao.

◄◄◄◄◄◄◄◄◄◄◄◄◄◄◄◄◄◄◄◄◄◄◄◄◄◄◄◄◄◄◄

The Rights of Spring